selected poetry

of
Cecilio García-Camarillo

Introduction by Enrique R. Lamadrid

Arte Público Press
Houston, Texas
2000

This volume is made possible through grants from the National Endowment for the Arts (a federal agency), Andrew W. Mellon Foundation, and the City of Houston through The Cultural Arts Council of Houston, Harris County.

PS

3557

-A711244

A6

2000

Recovering the past, creating the future

Arte Público Press
University of Houston
Houston, Texas 77204-2174

Cover design by Eclipse Design Group

García Camarillo, Cecilio.
  [Selections. 2000]
  Selected poetry of Cecilio García-Camarillo; with an introduction by Enrique R. Lamadrid.
     p. cm.
  ISBN 1-55885-281-6 (alk. paper)
  I. Mexican Americans—Poetry. I. Title.

PS3557.A711244 A6 2000
811'54—dc21   00-023272
                                                                           CIP

Introduction © 2000 by Enrique R. Lamadrid. Originally published, in slightly different form, in the *Dictionary of Literary Biography*, Volume 209 (1999); reprinted courtesy of the Gale Group.

0 1 2 3 4 5 6 7 8 9   10 9 8 7 6 5 4 3 2 1

Contents

Introduction

Enrique R. Lamadrid
University of New Mexico

POET, PUBLISHER, EDITOR, literary journalist, textual artist, script writer, radio personality, and cultural attaché, Cecilio García-Camarillo (September 12, 1943) is a complete Chicano Renaissance man, a gentle warrior whose cultural activism over the past quarter-century has transfigured Chicano literary culture. With seventeen bilingual chapbooks to his credit, his poetry is brash and playful, reso-nant with dream imagery, pulsating with dialogic orality, passionately involved with the personal dimensions of social struggle and the tortu-ous inner quest for self understanding. His command of the *poema breve* and affinity with the highly visual imagery of the haiku has also led him to explore concrete poetry and create over five hundred *poe-mas visuales*—poster-sized frames of text swirled into rivers and patterns that graphically recall the forces that created them. García-Camarillo's individual creative vision is profoundly articulated with his community. He founded and edited two influential reviews, *Magazín* (1971-1972) and *Caracol* (1974-1977), which provided a forum for scores of new Chicano writers. His newsletter *Rayas* (1978-1979) evolved into a weekly public radio show, "Espejos de Aztlán" (1979–present), the longest-running cultural affairs program at radio station KUNM in Albuquerque, New Mexico. His long association, as a scriptwriter, with La Compañía de Teatro de Albuquerque has also earned him a place in the history of bilingual community theatre.

In an editorial in a 1981 special issue of *Revista Río Bravo* dedicated to Cecilio García-Camarillo, editor Carlos Nicolás Flores offers a qualified indication of the esteem the poet-activist enjoys in the Chicano literary community:

> Though unknown in his hometown [Laredo], he is loved within the movement. Max Martínez described him in *Carta Abierta*, a literary newsletter circulated nationally among Chicano writers and artists, as "one of the most respected figures in the Chicano movement." Everywhere I have been in my recent travels as editor—Austin, Houston, San Antonio, Albuquerque, and so forth—I have found the same sentiments expressed towards him, affection and respect. In Houston, Inez Hernández Tovar, a Chicana poet from Galveston, remarked: "He never stops. He never loses faith. He keeps us going." In Austin, José Flores Peregrino, a Chicano poet from Laredo, said, "The people in the barrio respect him. And then he never loses his head. He is *so calm*." In Laredo, Father Roberto Peña, a priest at Our Lady of Guadalupe Church, commented: "An elegant and humane man—committed to *la raza*. He is indigenous, generous, and conscientious." Perhaps the most significant lesson those of us in Laredo can derive from these commentaries is that Laredo, despite its fashionable contempt for Chicanos and the Chicano movement in general, has produced in Cecilio García-Camarillo an important Chicano leader and thereby has contributed significantly (although unconsciously) to the development of this movement.
>
> *Revista Río Bravo* 1, 1 (Winter 1981): 19

Although his family always lived in Laredo, Texas, Cecilio García-Camarillo was delivered on September 12, 1943, by a *partera* in the nearby village of Big Wells where Julia Camarillo was kept during the traditional forty-day *cuarentena* period following childbirth. He is the oldest of five children, with two brothers and two sisters. His father, Mónico García, was away fighting in France and did not meet Cecilio until he was four years old, after the conclusion of World War II. The initial absence of the father turned into distance strained by alcohol and ultimately severed by strife between a proud veteran father and a son passionately opposed to the war in Vietnam. The retention of his mother's last name is a symbolic indication of her redemptive significance in Cecilio's life. After a lifetime of struggle with the anguished family dynamics that shaped his inner life, the mature poet recalls the excruciating scenes and exorcises the source of his pain in dream poem "4":

> I'm about 30
> as i stand by my father's deathbed
>
> he's got all kinds of tubes
> coming out of his wasted body
>
> gasping for breath
> he says he wants to have a final talk
> pero le contesto que no podemos
> porque no sabemos conversar
>
> i walk away quickly
> porque ahora sospecho
> que quiere cobrar venganza
> because he thinks i'm not his son
>
> when i'm about 19
> mamá dances in the livingroom
>
> le explico que su devotion
> to an alcoholic is irrational
>
> for the last time
> i'm asking you to leave him . . .
>
> i'm about 10
> and papá is getting ready
> to gamble in hell . . .
>
> when mamá calls him
> a drunken liar he hits her on the face
> y cuando cae al piso
> le da una patada
>
> mamá bleeds profusely
> and the boy walks away
>
> he wishes the moon

>   was not fat and shiny
>   so he could cry harder
>
>   it's always easier
>   to cry the heart out
>   in total darkness
>   *Dream Walking* 1994: 9-12

With the exception of one maternal grandfather from Zacatecas, both of the poet's families have been Tejano as long as anyone can guess: "It's not in our memory that we came from anywhere else." [All quotes from personal interview, February 27, 1995.] Although both his parents were migrant agricultural workers before the war, his father's job with the railroad was a ticket to another kind of life and a link to the urban culture of Chicago, where many family members went back and forth to work in factories. Riding the train and interpreting for his mother are among his earliest recollections:

> I can always remember travelling by train always running into Mexicanos that needed help, porque no dominaban el inglés. Ever since I can remember we would always be helping the Mexicanos to make phone calls, to ask for the food that they wanted to eat when we would get to the train stations . . .

Decades later, García-Camarillo continues his advocacy work for Mexicanos as a case worker and cultural attaché in the Mexican Consulate of Albuquerque.

Memories of a border childhood in Laredo's *barrio* del Trompezón also center around the importance of friends and the formative centrality of language in its bilingual complexity.

> Some of the things that I remember about those days was the great amistad that existed before between the guys. And this great awareness of language, because there was so much joking back and forth. Everything had double meaning. You had to defend yourself verbally, because you could be victimized pretty brutally, not actually physically, there wasn't any fighting, but verbally. And so I consider all that as an apprenticeship for later on developing an appreciation for poetry . . . There are several terms, albur, cábula, joking around. Those were the words we used. A lot of humor, a lot

of double meaning. I think it was very creative. We spent a lot of time playing with language, with English, and doing things with language, reinventing language, more or less.

García-Camarillo developed his literary interests as an English major at the University of Texas at Austin from 1967 to 1971; his classmates there included anthropologist José Limón and historian David Montejano. In 1970 he published his first poem, winning the American Academy of Poets annual contest, an award won by subsequently Montejano the following year.

Cecilio's creative impulse exploded with the tragedy and contradictions of the Vietnam War and the conflict it caused in his own family. In line to be drafted, his personal response to protest the war was an extended hunger strike, the physical consequences of which he still endures. His 1971 poem "Canción" is a personal manifesto and incantation for peace and for the strength to resist:

> camina en sí
> camina en sí
>
> porque no tiene patria
>   presidente
>   iglesia
>   o dinero
>
> camina en sí
> camina en sí
>
> con 122 libras de conciencia
>   contra la guerra
>   de los gringos
>   en vietnam
>
> camina en sí
> camina en sí
>
> porque es chicano
>   de aztlán
>   y habla caló
>
> camina en sí

camina en sí . . .

cargando
  las gruesas contradicciones
  de chavo colonizado
  en su huelga de hambre . . .
      Carambola 1982: 3-4

During this difficult period his primary nourishment was poetry itself, the poems of surrealist anguish and social commitment of Pablo Neruda and of the post-World War II poets of Japan, whose strength in the face of despair and oblivion was poetry itself. García-Camarillo dedicated several poems to César Chávez, whose fasts were concurrent with his own.

As the danger of his own dilemma subsided, he rededicated himself to the Chicano movement and began the business of creating a literary legacy. In San Antonio he founded and published *Magazín*, a pioneer Chicano literary review that enjoyed a run of fourteen issues in 1971 and 1972.

> I was always combining literatura with politics. It was very important and it served as an organizing tool. A lot of awareness was spreading, el concepto de Aztlán, la identificación con la raíz indígena . . . People were demanding that education be relevant to their own experiences . . . It was like a new level of awareness of who we were . . . Our job is to create a solid foundation of literatura, something that will not disappear tomorrow or the day after, but something that is big and solid and strong. And something that will endure . . .

After a brief sojourn in Toronto, García-Camarillo returned to San Antonio and began publishing the successor to *Magazín*, called *Caracol* (1974–1977). Many Chicano poets and critics still active today published some of their first pieces in *Caracol*. Creative writing was accepted from all sectors, including community people, high-school students, and prison inmates. Numerous articles on the important political events of the times show the intimate linkage between social and cultural activism that marks this first dynamic period of the Chicano literary renaissance. In the poet's words:

Caracol became an important forum for a lot of things. It was during those times that the Texas farmworkers were doing their strikes in Texas. The situation with high schools had accelerated and exploded, there were walkouts all over the place. Police brutality was just really bad. And of course also those were the times that El Partido de la Raza Unida became a prominent force . . . We were open to everything and everyone. Always supporting las mujeres también . . . And so, with all these things happening and we were right in the middle of it with the little revistita *Caracol* . . . There's no university that could give you a tenth of the education that it did . . . It was difficult to put out a monthly magazine, it was no easy task, it was very draining, but we were young and reckless and full of energy . . . Everyone was such a great supporting cast . . . But really the major forces behind that were myself and my wife Mía and we worked very hard. People like Max Martínez, like César Martínez, like Reyes Cárdenas, like Angela de Hoyos, they were also very helpful . . . We used IBM [typewriter]s and took it to a big printing company there in San Antonio . . . It was just a small rag, but we were sending it to every major university in this country. And then we had a following in Europe. We would send it to Germany, to France, and to Spain, those were the three main countries. We don't know how they got a hold of those, but they would subscribe. And then, of course, we would send it south, to México, as far as Chile and Argentina. We used to send it to Nicaragua, we sent it to Cuba. We didn't print that many, but it just went all over.

Caracol had a literary impact which far surpassed its actual circulation (one thousand copies) and regional base. An interesting register of the breadth of *Caracol*'s literary audience was a trilingual English/ Spanish/ Náhuatl poetry contest announced in the magazine in the fall of 1976. The result was a 1977 anthology, *Nahualliandoing*. The title springs from a Náhuatl term for animal spirit guide, transformed with Spanish and English suffixes into a gerund implying both the linguistic and spiritual aspirations of the poems. First honors and one hundred dollars applauded the untitled poem of José Antonio Burciaga, a California poet and humorist whose subsequent literary fame extends to the present. Second prize and fifty dollars was sent to Utah to Chicano poet-warrior Abelardo Delgado with his poem "Mictlán." Third place and a twenty-five dollar award went to California poet Rebecca Huerta for "Yotl With Nature." Of the twenty-three Chicano poets published, seven were women and sixteen

men, and the geographic distribution was fourteen from Texas, five
from California, two from Chicago, and one each from New York and
Chicago. Other literary notables in *Nahualliandoing* include Octavio
Romano, Reyes Cárdenas, José Montalvo, Carlos Cortez, Carlos
Cumpián, Jacinto Jesús Cardona, Joe Olvera, and Ronnie Burk. The
panel of judges, besides Cecilio and his Norwegian-American wife
Mía Stageberg, is also worthy of mention: Tomás Rivera, Angela de
Hoyos, Evangelina Vigil, Max Martínez, and Alfredo and Susana de
la Torre. In his trilingual prologue, Cecilio notes:

> Parece que anda pegando fuerte la onda de consciencia lingüística.
> Parece que ya le andamos escarbando más hondo a la raíz pa' tratar
> de conocernos mejor. Chicano acceptance of Náhuatl es dirección
> positiva. It's a good way to pegarle de aquellas a algo más íntimo,
> más netamente Chicano. Chanza que con 3 idiomas le estamos sien-
> do más fieles a nuestro espíritu y a nuestra compleja realidad
> Chicana.

The Chicano poet best known for multilingual poetry does not appear
in this anthology, though he probably was aware of it, for in the pre-
vious year (1976), Alurista himself provides a critical prologue to *Get
Your Tortillas Together*, García-Camarillo's first book of poems, an
honor shared with fellow Tejano poets Carmen Tafolla and Reyes
Cárdenas. Alurista's response springs from the same poetic coordi-
nates as the poems themselves:

> Cecilio García-Camarillo [*et al.*] journeys across intimate timespace
> eventos para narrar un tiempoespacio histórico y colectivo amasan-
> do tortillas míticas que desuedan el mundo del bolillo las
> apariencias se derriten in counterpointed hechos and appearances
> disappear their tone is machete clad and razor sharp su lenguaje es
> cotidiano even though it draws from the multidimensional tongue
> which xicanos have carved out of spanish and english.

The poems themselves percolate with the same clever dramatic irony
that characterizes much of García-Camarillo's subsequent work. The
lead poem, "Sala," equates the labor of poetry with that of the fields:

la sala es como un acre
de tierra harada,
lista pa la siembra.

las semillas:
una mesa donde reposa el sol,
tres brujos callados
con sombreros de pico,
una lámpara que parece
chicharra,
y un collar de ojos
de venado.

se asoma mi ruca
y me trai el sombrero

voy a regar
la sala.

Get Your Tortillas Together (1976): 7

The seeds to be sown for the harvest of poetry are a sunny table, three enigmatic figures in peaked hats, a lamp, and a necklace of deer's eyes, a large black-and-red seed used in Mexico for cures and good-luck charms. The conversational diction "pa, trai" and caló jargon "ruca" are also trademarks of García-Camarillo's colloquial style.

Other "tortillas" from the collection include a series of ten numbered "Event" poems which place the poetic persona in a Dada-esque series of situations and dilemmas. "Event 5" humorously connects mundane Chicano reality to the mythic dimension of the Aztec world at the time of European conquest:

make some instant coffee
and sit on the porch

pretend you are
Moctezuma and that
the mailman is a
messenger from
your friend the King of Texcoco . . .

Get Your Tortillas Together (1976): 22

The implied message is the Chicano discovery of classical Náhuatl esthetics, in *xochitl,* in *cuicatl* the flowersongs of the poet king Netzahualcóyotl.

García-Camarillo's personal discovery of the symbology of the larger Chicano poetic landscape coincides with the birth (August 5, 1975) and naming of his first child and future poet, Itz-Ollín (itz = obsidian, ollín = movement). "Event 7" is a chronicle of a new father's joy and self-sacrifice:

> put your ear
> up to your new-born
> baby's heart
>
> and collect his
> heartbeats
>
> take your ear
> off and put it
> in an incenseburner
>
> shaped like a quetzal-bird
>
> light up the heartbeats
> and rest assured
> that the aroma
>
> will be even
> more precious
> than copal

Get Your Tortillas Together (1976): 24

In his prologue, Alurista comments on one of the "haiku" from the "tortillas" collection:

> . . .y con humor negro Cecilio se jacta de todo cualquier dogma se desvanece ante su cabulera metáfora que afirma la espontaniedad del ser his descriptions of the concrete does not rule out mythical timespace but often snakes out his own, personalizing history and legend in familiar spheres que se contienen sí mismas

la lluvia
es como Emiliano Zapata:
ojos sin fin

Get Your Tortillas Together (1976): 5

In his early work, García-Camarillo revels in the symbols and syntax of Chicano cultural nationalism—revolutionary heroes, Aztec indigenism, English-Spanish code switching, and *barrio* slang.

Late in the same remarkable bicentennial year that Cecilio got his "Tortillas" together, he lent his inexhaustible editorial energy to a landmark encyclopedic collection of Chicano writing in Texas. *El Quetzal Emplumece* includes a broad sampling of the writings of teachers, church activists, community organizers, and both obscure and emerging Chicano writers, many of whom are still prominent decades later. In a personal statement preceding a series of Quetzalcoatl poems in this collection, García-Camarillo declares himself Tejano to the core, but confesses his ambition to travel all of Aztlán to know himself and his people better.

Although the goal of his pilgrimage of the summer of 1977 was Arizona, García-Camarillo succeeded in getting his family only as far as New Mexico, destined to become the poet's center space and permanent home, "por el resto de mi vida." Soon after settling in Albuquerque, García-Camarillo resumed his cultural journalism with *Rayas* for another two exhausting but fulfilling years as editor (1978-1979) before directing his communal energies into the immediate, oral dimensions of radio. Except for his personal archive of selected broadcasts of "Espejos de Aztlán" over fifteen years, this chronicle is ultimately ephemeral, although thousands of listeners will attest to the immense impact of the weekly show on the cultural and political scene in Albuquerque.

Besides his cultural journalism, the other high-profile literary work that García-Camarillo has engaged in is community theatre. His long association with La Compañía de Teatro de Albuquerque and one of its directors, Ramón Flores, began in 1983 with *Vista del Puente,* a bilingual translation-adaptation of Arthur Miller's *View from the Bridge.* Other playwrights adapted for bilingual Chicano productions include Moliere, Machiavelli, Dickens, Manuel Méndez Ballester, and Estela Portillo Trambley. García-Camarillo has received significant recognition in local theatre reviews for making these plays accessible, interesting, and lively. The most original play in this theatrical collaboration and the poet's most significant dramatic writing is in *La Virgen de Tepeyac* (1992), a humorous and political thriller which García-Camarillo co-wrote with Ramón Flores. Theater critic Catalina Reyes praises:

> ... some particularly snappy writing, especially in scenes where the Aztec characters interact. Here the co-writers delightfully achieve that elusive balance of idea and whimsy that communicates strong messages without the viewer feeling clubbed. Among those messages is one about the history of oppressed people undermining their own battle to survive by fighting among themselves; and another about how only through the end of such infighting can people support each other enough to stand up to the social results of oppression ...
>
> *Albuquerque Journal*, December 19, 1992

Over the years, García-Camarillo has worked in a variety of jobs, with hospitals and non-profit associations such as a community food bank, where his work as a truck driver did not interfere with his poetic endeavor, because you can write a haiku "even while shifting gears. I wrote a lot of haiku in the streets of Albuquerque," the poet admits. His work with cultural organizations includes positions with Pajarito Publications (with José Armas), the Hispanic Culture Foundation, and ultimately, the Mexican Consulate. Important recognition of his ongoing poetic career came in 1982 with a National Endowment for the Arts Fellowship, which also allowed him to buy a house in Atrisco, in Albuquerque's South Valley.

This domestic space and its inhabitants are as central in the poet's work as in his personal life. Cecilio García-Camarillo's daughters were born in Albuquerque: Cielo Rojo (March 7, 1978), whose name derives from Mayan calendar; and Oraibi (August 22, 1980), named for the ancient Hopi village. After a ten-year relationship, Mía Stageberg and the poet went their separate ways, putting him in the unanticipated role of single father. His professional teaching certificate is an indication of his interest in cultivating the young. Although he has never been a teacher, the poet became an extraordinary mentor to his children. He is so intuitively attuned to the minds and feelings of children that they quite naturally became a major inspiration in his own creative imagination. Therefore, the three children merit much more than passing biographical attention. All three began by exploring their dreams with their father and by illustrating with fanciful line drawings his poetic response to their imaginations.

At age four, Itz-Ollín and his father collaborated on a children's story that became *Cuervos en el Río Grande* in 1983, a mythic story of migrating crows on the banks of the same river that the poet-father knew as a child in Laredo, a thousand miles south. Itz-Ollín went on to publish several other bilingual children's stories including *El volcán de la dragona* (1982), *El perro fiero de la acequia* (1982), *Una mañana extraña* (1982), *La casa del brujo* (1984), *Pepe el piano* (1986), all with Mano Izquierda Books. He finished his first novel at the age of fifteen, although it is as yet unpublished.

Cecilio's collaboration with his older daughter, Cielo Rojo, produced *Pajarita* in 1984, a bilingual story with whimsical drawings designed to teach a child to read Spanish. The heroine dreams she is a many-colored bird who flies above the world to understand it better through her extraordinary senses. The story emphasizes trusting in the power of the imagination. In 1994, Cielo published a first collection of poems, *Blue Innocence*, which tempers lyrical themes with the worldly realities of betrayal, abortion, gang warfare, and death.

At age seven, Cecilio's younger daughter, Oraibi, sat her father down and told him the story that became *Black Horse on the Hill* (1988), a tale of a solitary horse visited by five pesky crows. The drawings rival those of Oraibi's sister and brother for their freshness and ingenuity.

In Albuquerque, the labors of creative writing and publishing converged for García-Camarillo with his own Mano Izquierda Books, an ongoing collection of over two dozen chapbooks, illustrated with original drawings and clip-art, and offset printed in limited (but successive) editions of one hundred. They are distributed locally at bookstores, by mail order, at book fairs and poetry readings, and by the poet personally to a large circle of friends, family, and literary allies. García-Camarillo has poured all his literary energy into Mano Izquierda since 1981, making it the longest-running series of chapbooks in Chicano literary history. The modest print runs do not faze the poet, who is more concerned with creative continuity and quality than with literary celebrity. In any case, the history of Chicano poetry is not complete without careful consideration of this major poet.

An interesting index of García-Camarillo's thirteen chapbooks published from 1981 to the present is available in the words of the poet-as-critic of his own work. This succinct recapitulation is from the same interview with the poet quoted above:

> Two currents run through my work. One is experimental stuff that continues traditions that started around the turn of the century that I think was one of the most fertile periods in terms of global creativity. It's interesting how a lot of these things are related to wars. But the works that the surrealists, that the dadaists, all those things, I kind of inherited those things . . . Then at the same time doing social realism. I'm able to do both things . . .

More specifically, the reflections quoted below (after book titles) are from the prefatory cover notes on the back of each book. Curiously, García-Camarillo wrote the first eleven in an authoritative critical third-person, but in the last two he takes off the mask and shares his first-person comments. Since these chapbooks are not in many libraries, it is useful to quote the cover notes here to get an overview of the trajectory of García-Camarillo's poetry over the last twenty-five years.

The most convenient stylistic cataloging of García-Camarillo's poetry conveniently corresponds to its geographic provenance. Although all of the chapbooks were published in Albuquerque, the first six (*Hang a Snake, Ecstasy and Puro Pedo, Winter Month, Calcetines Embotellados, Double Face,* and *Carambola*) were written in Texas in the early 1970s while the prolific young poet was discovering his muse. All these poems share a experimental vanguard spirit and short line structure, replete with visual imagery, and an ambiguous first-person poetic voice whose presence in the text often creates a dimension of dramatic irony.

[*Hang a Snake* (1981) — cover notes]

. . . a collection of 20 poems written in 1970 and early 71 at El Quiote, García-Camarillo's family farm near the Mexican border city of Laredo, Texas. The Chicano spiritual crisis in a rural context is the explicit theme of this text which actually reads as a lengthy,

bilingual poem. García-Camarillo utilizes the technique of halluci-
nation as the basis for his portrayal of a self-doubting voice,
fractured cultural traditions, and a pain-inflicting South Texas envi-
ronment.

These line-centered poems in the setting of the family *ranchito* are
decentered spiritually. In an ironic pastoral mode, the poet returns to
the *campo* in a vain search for his origins. Urban anxieties unwind
only to reveal another level of bleakness and desperation. In "rancho"
the poet asks himself:

> a qué le tiras
> crouching todo el día
>   on this sandpapered land
> of malnutritioned shrubs
>
>   la luna
> parece una tuerca
>   de plastic
>
>   my soul
> well
> there's plastic in it too
>
>   city acid has galloped
> through veins
> and you've let a few books
>   curdle your mind cells . . .
> *Hang a Snake* (1981): 4

Intense introspection eventually leads, through hallucination, to frag-
mentation of the poetic self in "Presence of a Poem."

>   . . .your eyes
> are a grasshopper that jumps around
> and lands on an ashbrown shrub
>
>   rubs shiny legs
> & disperses ripples of explosions
>
>   flips wings

> & jars loose brown silk dust
>
> > to its countless eyes
> > the on-coming night
> > is whirlpools
> > of emotion . . .
> > *Hang a Snake* (1981): 28

The next collection of poems, from approximately the same period, takes several steps further into minimalism. The *ars poética* manifesto for *Ecstasy and Puro Pedo* is a Dionysian invitation to poetic excess and linguistic sacrifice:

> to ecstasy
> y puro pedo
>
> i commit
> the senses
>
> i criminal
> water the words
> then bleed the words
>
> water the sun
> then erase the sun
>
> i
> & xerox copy of myself
> > *Ecstasy and Puro Pedo* (1981): 4

The preface to this 1981 collection is a poem in itself:

> *Ecstasy and Puro Pedo*
> is a viaje estrambólico
> in which Chicano relaje,
> Aztlán rural existentialism,
> dadaist poetic irreverence,
> haiku compactness,
> and radio splicing techniques
> are twisted together to create a knotted,
> introverted portrait of the Chicano experience
> in the States.

In this collection of 12 poems
written between 1970-71,
the experimental underlying tissue in
García-Camarillo's poetry really comes into focus.

A full blown *flor y canto* Chicano poetics is evident in this collection, which is complete with allusions to classical Náhuatl themes such as the hummingbird, a warrior spirit that brings blessings down from heaven.

hummingbird baila
en árbol de la vida

hummingbird
picotea
2 canciones
2 arcoirises
de la máscara

flag of duality
snakes in my heart

snake
hides in the void
of the heart

el cielo
tiene un agujero

void
of the land

el cielo
esconde su agujero
del olvido

hummingbird
pierces the void
of the eyes

Ecstasy and Puro Pedo (1981): 11

The next collection steps away from the ecstatic into a more severe minimalism set in the same disenchanted pastoral setting as *Hang a Snake*. *Winter Month* (1982) is a bleak thirty-poem chronicle reflecting the season as well as the anguish that has overcome the poet.

> *Winter Month*
> may be the first collection of haiku
> published by a Chicano poet.
> García-Camarillo
> immerses himself in the spirit
> rather than the traditional, metrical form of haiku
> in an attempt to pull together his center,
> fragmented by the harsh South Texas environment
> and the brutalizing forces of American culture.
> Using psychiatric jargon,
> he struggles to transcend his own alienated
> and cynical voice.
> This is the 3rd edition of *Winter Month*,
> which originally formed part of a diary
> that the author kept in 1970.
> Along with *Ecstasy* and *Puro Pedo* and *Hang a Snake*,
> it was written when García-Camarillo lived at his
> family's farm, El Quiote, near Laredo, Texas.

A certain greyness, tedium, and despair mark all these poems:

> a photograph-stillness
> if the poem doesn't move
> all is dead
> > 11/29/1970
>
> nature
> a brief irregular grey image
> a compulsion to keep secrets
>
> > 11/30/1970
> > *Winter Month* (1982): 30-31

The next collection is an innovative exercise in recovery, a revising of poems written a full decade earlier accompanied by responses, or extended glosses, written long after. The curious image of bottled poems and bottled socks appears in many poems.

[*Calcetines embotellados* (1982)—cover notes]

... haunting, internal landscape reminiscent of the poetry of post-war Japan. Lyrically, los unsupressed cucuys tienen la rienda suelta para danzar por todos los parameters of his poetic vision. The integrity lies in the acceptance of these feelings projected mostly in chicano-type Spanish que fueron escritos en 1970-71. *Calcetines embotellados* is an experiment of transformations: the original (left side) poems, years later, became the right side animals that look, smell and behave somewhat like the sombras originales.

The monstrous animals or *cucuys* that lurk in these pages are carried in nightmarish images which recur from poem to poem, written almost entirely in Spanish. Empty streets, red lightbulbs, dogs dragging their entrails, rivers of filth, plastic skin, and the pen as a wriggling cockroach combine and recombine in a panoply reminiscent of the bleak surrealism of Pablo Neruda's *Residencias en la tierra*:

> un animal
> se traga la pintura
> roja del silencio
>
> la onda es de encuerar
> los sentimientos
> y escribirlos
>
> pero se engarruñan los dedos
> ante la inmensidad de la página
>
> la pluma
> es un cucaracho pataleando
>
> si quemo el pilar
> que sostiene el resorte
> de la noche
> se cae la luna como un cuchillo
>
> flotan en un río
> automóviles podridos
> como microbios
> en una llaga
>
> la mente es un foco rojo
> calentando las piernas de una mujer

Calcetines embotellados (1982): 9

This *ars poética* is a virtual journal of nightmares. The technique of vision and revision comes to the forefront again and with even more specificity in *Double-Face* (1982), in which the poet reaches the depth of cynicism and despair over the Vietnam War. The original poems were written in 1970, the companion poems in 1975, and the collection was rediscovered by the poet in 1980.

> *Double-Face* is García-Camarillo's most spiritually disturbing collection of poems. Doubt and isolation son las inquietudes que his haunting, bilingual voice dibuja en una configuración que es distressful as it is compelling. There is no escape from his godless universe, and one is condemned to alienation from the environment and from oneself. García-Camarillo methodically develops an abbreviated language para construir his crystal clear images of despair. Poetry of essentials, *Double Face* es una lucha que insiste on being heard.

The poet feels obliged to offer a page-long epilogue, explaining his despair:

> . . . the early '70s was a period of national disintegration and intense spiritual conflicts brought about by the viet-nam war. i was drawn inward and there too i faced the nightmare of my own monsters. I frankly can't relate much to these poems . . . now that *Double-Face* is finished, I just feel an incredible sense of relief.

The poems themselves offer a penetrating insight into the mind of the poet who responds to and clarifies his own despair in a jungle of symbolic imagery.

en pozos	en pozos
de víboras	donde descanzan víboras
	se mutilan estrellas
estrellas se mutilan	
y se baña	lo negro
lo negro	de noche
con cuernos	tiene cuernos que raspan
de propane gas	sensibilidad endrogada
por intestinos	un pensamiento
de ilusión	es largartijo-arcoiris
lagartijos	that diffuses to other planets
diffuse pa otros planetas	

río que surces	succulent río
tierra	hondo en vida
inflada	inflado de mentiras
de mentiras	llévame contingo
te burlas	desde túnel
con colmillos de espejos	le ladro a gente
y cuernos remoliniando	con dientes de azufre
y deste agujero	con cuervo
como ojo	en espalda
de cuervo	con espuma
malparido	en boca
	muerdo canción
yo ladro	que no se puede terminar
a la gente	

Double-Face (1982): 10-11

The next collection spans the entire decade. The feverish poetic pro-
duction of 1970 and 1971 gives way to a more measured pace, which
carries clear signs of the evolution and maturation of a poet.
Carambola (1982) is a reunion of poems which precede and follow
Get Your Tortillas Together through 1979. In these pages the poet
emerges from the rarified discourse of despair, identifies its source,
and joins with others to combat it.

> *Carambola* is a serious billiard game, and in this collection of 12
> poems that span 10 years, García-Camarillo plays with the various
> levels of Chicano language in an attempt to get to the heart of the
> two major movements in his life: the oneiric and the socio-political.
> Se vale.

The poem "Canción," already cited, is a good example of the uplifting
strength the poet summons to confront and overcome the forces
against him. He curses the war in Vietnam as he challenges it with
fasting and a spiritual diet of words. "Preparándonos pa la marcha de
Muleshoe a Austin, Tejas 1.27" is a chronicle of the Texas farmwork-
ers' march on the capital to demand their rights. The poem ends with
shouts of "ya basta / ya basta" (28). Yet, even the most overtly politi-
cal of García-Camarillo's poems are playfully revolutionary in their
form, as in "Tarde y Patas":

tarde esqueletuda

> tierruda
> enfermuda
> putuda
> pobresuda
> mugresuda
> lagrimuda
> colonizuda

patas con callos

> con cansancio
> con silencio
> con hambre
> con tristeza
> con dolor
> con coraje
> con carabinas
> con revolución

Carambola (1982): 14

The ludic element in García-Camarillo's poetry is back in force in *Carambola* and is especially evident in poems such as "Sapos" (pp. 24-25), in which the entire landscape comes alive with toads and ends with the poet himself turning into a *sapo* and hopping down an alley.

As is evident by the quick succession of the chapbooks discussed above, much of the poet's energy in his first Albuquerque years was spent publishing earlier work, editing *Rayas*, and working with Pajarito Publications (for the duration of *Rayas*), which published books, anthologies, and the Chicano literary journal *De Colores*. The first poems written in New Mexico are published in *Burning Snow*, a collection of "haiku" which stand in sharp contrast to the *Winter Month* "haiku" set in south Texas. Like their Texas predecessors, these poems are linked to a season characterized by retreat, contemplation, and keeping warm. But in the second collection, the dreary grey landscapes of the southern Rio Grande valley are replaced by the dazzling snowy landscapes of the headwaters of the same river. These are the poet's extensive prefatory reflections, which stand in curious contrast to the brevity of the poems themselves:

[*Burning Snow* (1984) — cover notes]

Written around the Christmas holidays in 1983, *Burning Snow* is García-Camarillo's second collection of published haiku. Once again he opts for the Japanese poetic form of economy of words, focus on a particular season, depth of image and clarity of vision to portray his inner landscape and this time not his ancestral land at the Mexican border near Laredo, Texas, but the landscape around the D. H. Lawrence Ranch, north of Taos, New Mexico. García-Camarillo's feelings are the protagonist that journey from being nauseously trapped in the city, brooding over the decaying body and crumpled spirit, detesting the aloneness of the aging process, to the rural, open spaces where acceptance of fate and communion with the sun and snow is accessible. In-between these two poles of the soul, his children, several women, animals and even insects visit with García-Camarillo, and he draws them all with the finesse and honesty that is his distinctive style.

There is less desperation in these northern landscapes. Somehow the pain is more completely integrated or absorbed into them:

> the snow falling from the trees
> makes me feel
> like i'm not alone
>
> *Burning Snow* (1984): 18

> the crows & i
> pace up & down
> the river we like so much
>
> *Burning Snow* (1984): 14

The anguish of distant urban landscapes is quelled by the mountain stillness. The links and reminders of the *barrio* are softened:

> so many
> electrical wires
> so where's the spider   *Burning Snow* (1984): 4

the drunk's eyes
are redder
than a rose

Burning Snow (1984): 14

The poet's strongest mythical and personal link to New Mexico is geo-
graphic—the Rio Grande itself. The following conversation with the
river "Talking to the Rio Grande" was written in 1983:

Siempre regreso a ti, my source, you gnarled piece of liquid leather.
When I feel good or reventado you're always there for me.
Solamente your indifference tiene la capacidad de entender the out-
pourings of my soul. As a child in Laredo I knew you as the
powerful divider of a people who were once one and the same, y
ahora de aquel lado están los mexicanos, y acá, nosotros, los tejanos.
You flowed on doing your thing, not caring about the weird games
men play. I swam in you and your dark waters mixed with my blood.
Toda mi vida he permanecido cerca de ti cause I have the need to
reveal myself to you so that I can cope con todas las chingaderas de
la vida. Listen to me old one, and help me make her love me once
again.

Crickets (1992): 18

The subsequent New Mexico poems are characterized by longer and
longer poetic lines, longer poems, and further development of rhetor-
ical features such as incantatory structure and poetic dialogues.

With his *Borlotes mestizos*, the social vein of García-Camarillo's
poetry reaches its apex. If *alborotar* means to rile up or infuriate, the
borlote is a caló expression denoting occasion for outrage, the impas-
sioned complaint of the *mestizo,* marginalized underdog of society.

[*Borlotes mestizos* (1984)— cover notes]

At a time when Chicano academicians are making their move to put
bureaucratic suits and ties on carefully crafted poetry with near to
nothing content, García-Camarillo's *Borlotes mestizos* reasserts la
meta fundamental de nuestra literatura: opinar concretamente sobre
nuestra realidad. García-Camarillo's voice cruises powerfully
through the plight of laborers, the contradictions of Reagan's poli-
tics, police brutality, la concientización de los pintos, colonialism in
Texas agribusiness, la amargura de stereotyping, the business of tor-

turing in El Salvador, personal weaknesses and the everpresent dangers of being a Chicano in the USA. It is a voice that consciously reaches back to the oral tradition of storytelling pa contarnos trozos de la vida que nosotros conocemos tan bien.

A heightened narrative sense emerges in these poems, fueled by personal reactions to the controversies of the 1980s. The link between the personal and the political is the body itself, the corporeal site of political repression, as the testimonials of Central American torture victims confirm. In "Cuerpo Humano," the poet links his own body to the suffering and launches incantations of protest:

>   el cuerpo humano de carne
>   atacado por metal
>   el cuerpo humano de carne
>   atacado por vidrio
>   el cuerpo humano de carne
>   atacado por lumbre
>   el cuerpo humano de carne
>   atacado por madera . . .
>
>   como duele al cuerpo humano
>   cuando el enemigo
>   corta una cruz en el estómago
>   con una botella quebrada de coca cola . . .
>
>   y es el cuerpo humano de carne
>   donde nacen y se guardan
>   las ideas
>   de liberación
>   de justicia
>   igualdad
>   y amor
>
>   y por eso a veces
>   los militares
>   los religiosos
>   presidentes
>   y vendidos
>   torturan
>   con metal
>   con vidrio

> lumbre
> y madera
> el cuerpo humano . . .

Borlotes mestizos (1984): 35-38

Gone is the hallucinatory anguish fueled by the war in Vietnam. Here is a clarity fueled by rage and a desire to enlist language to resist oppression.

Another poem, "Ojos de Rata," refuses to take the compassion of the reader for granted. Ojos de Rata is a *barrio* character who becomes a victim of police brutality. With a kind of Brechtian alienation effect, Ojos de Rata is distanced from any easy sympathy. His story is told in *barrio* slang as an animal fable. As he cruises Albuquerque's South Valley, he is stopped and killed by a pack of dogs (with badges):

> . . . el ojos de rata
> cranked up the ranfla
> tuned his radio de kabq
> and sings along to a rola
> by little joe y la familia
> esa que dice algo de que todos
> traemos la virgen de guadalupe
> en el pecho . . .
>
> de volada lo pararon
> y chanza que cuando le hecharon
> la luz del flashlight
> en los ojos
> al ojos de rata
> the animal instinct de los perros
> was confirmed to the max
>
> right on
> aquí 'stá the perfect
> saturday night south valley greaser
> those eyes
> tell us he's up to no good
> chingao que ojos tan feos
> parece que te los regaló el diablo cabrón

Borlotes mestizos (1984): 13-18

Also from the early 1980s is a poem titled *The Line*, which occupies an entire chapbook. It is a chronicle of humiliation, solidarity, and frustration, a compendium of impressions and emotions felt by the poet while getting food stamps.

[*The Line* (1984)—cover notes]

Written in the winter of 1981, *The Line* is to date García-Camarillo's longest poem. It represents a general statement on the problem of hunger in the U.S., and more concretely, an on the spot poetic portrayal of typical bureaucratic foul-ups that literally leave the poor, old and unemployed out in the cold with empty stomachs. García-Camarillo, as a participant of the food stamp line, narrates with succinct immediacy the tragi-comic raw energy of los de abajo. The voice is haikulike, bold and conversational in its strokes that cut out a vision of a group's will to survive. Literatura social y comprometida: García-Camarillo logra superar el yo que escribe solamente lo que yo siento. Conscious of his own socio-economic status, se atreve a tomar la responsabilidad de recoger the collective feelings of los marginados. The freezing winter day is as much a participant in this drama of controlled violence and transcendence as are the real and memorable characters that move up and down the strangely formed food stamp line. But if there is one protagonist in *The Line*, it is el sentimiento de compasión that permeates the very soul of the poem.

Scene 5 describes an unusual encounter which in the barrio can occur any day of the week:

a 60 year old pachuco
with greased hair combed back
and a centipede-looking scar on his forehead
offers a 2 year old giggly girl some candy

but the mother
with the nicest smile
says no sir
it's just too early for that garbage

The Line (1984): 8

After waiting in the freezing weather for hours, the poet receives stamps for another month's food:

> but we can't talk now
>
> the group is called again
> and in a sort of icy daze we wait some more
> in this big stuffy totally empty room
> that i immediately associate with concentration camps
>
> but anyway
> i join the crowd in smiling hotly
> with the smell of victory
> just behind a big glass window
>
> they call us again
> and i get $173 for the month
>
> i take a deep breath
> and head home
> through the lines of my people
> still waiting it out
> shoving
> cussing
> laughing
> joking
> refusing to surrender to the deadly cold
> in this our daily struggle for survival
>
> *The Line* (1984): 19

In his subsequent collection, *Zafa'o*, García-Camarillo paints a frenetic series of poetic portraits, tributes, and snapshots of a series of important people and portentous moments in his life.

[*Zafa'o* (1992) — cover notes]

> . . . explores through a 7 year tour de force the configurations of life's disillusionments as well as the enigmatic strength that propels us on. The 11 English/Spanish/bilingual imagistic poems are drawn with unparalleled intensity, not in his usual compact style, but in broader conversational strokes. García-Camarillo's mature voice is less cynical than accepting of the new and recurring pains that visit

and oftentimes stay to haunt us. *Zafa'o*, slang for crazy, unbalanced, free, may be García-Camarillo's most compelling and intimate poetry chapbook to date.

The book opens on an alarming and excruciating note with the poem titled "pig memory," a desperate and defensive response to a painful barb, undoubtedly something like "sexist macho pig," from the poet's significant other:

> . . . and your knifewords plunge
> into my gut then rip
> to spill my insides . . .
>
> . . . and as you start skinning me
> i ask you que no cortes la cabeza
> porque allí cargo la memoria
> de todo lo bello que he visto
> no cortes la cabeza . . .
>
> . . . pero debes considerar
> que ser marrano a veces no es decisión personal
> puede ser herencia o destino
> quizás así me formó la sociedad . . .
> *Zafa'o* (1992): 3-5

Without complaint or excuse, the penitent male accepts the cloak of blame, endures vivisection, wishing instead to be a horse, "and gallop locamente without impediments/ until I gradually dissolve."

As his personal life enters into a period of crisis, the poet uses the power of his art on himself, confronting the demons of his past and present. Intense emotional pain turns to loss and regret. All the decisive moments are recalled and lamented. This collection also includes a touching tribute to the poet's mother and a memorial for the death of his friend, New Mexican activist and graphic artist Rini Templeton.

These poems loosen all of the bonds of sanity and normalcy that it took so many years to construct. *Zafa'o* is an anticipation of the painful reckoning to come, a therapeutic disgorging of the misery of separation and loss that burst forth in the next book, the enigmatically titled *Crickets*.

[*Crickets* (1992) — cover notes]

. . . an experimental literary collage where social realism is woven with dream and metaphor to create a complex drama of probing ontological/social/spiritual anxieties. An interview with a barrio philosopher published years ago in "Caracol," a car conversation with an old hitch-hiker, a letter never mailed to a professor of sociology, a taped counseling session with a Chicano political theoretician, and a monologue written on the banks of the Rio Grande form the five narrative threads that García-Camarillo interlaces around the central theme of the text: the disintegration of his intense ten year relationship with his wife.

In these linked selections of narrative prose, the bitter and stressful anecdotes of separation are divulged. Solace is sought in revelation, reliance on the sage advice of strangers, and the Siddhartha-like conversation with the Rio Grande cited above. The crickets are from a nightmarish boyhood episode on the family farm. A group of boys find a dry well with snakes at the bottom, which they kill with volleys from their .22 rifles. They force the poet to descend on a rope to get the dead snakes. On the way down he discovers that the walls of the well are crawling with thousands of crickets. The imagery of this strange episode echoes in poems from different periods in the poet's life.

One look at the latest chapters of the poetic development of García-Camarillo reveals the poetic effects of this personal catharsis. Beyond pain, the chains fall away, and the maturing poet finds his fullest expressive voice. In *Fotos*, personal pain and desire are detached from anecdote, abstracted from memory, and explored in the medium of allegory and metaphor.

[*Fotos* (1993) — cover notes]

. . . empezó con las notas que escribí después de haber visto un libro de fotografía contemporánea de España. En el transcurso de 2 años I "layered" los textos con personal dreams and with influences from movies, Jung, the I Ching, Krishnamurti, and with work I've done for Chicano theatre. No estoy seguro si conozco a las mujeres de los poemas, pero me imagino que existen. I understood recently that what I was trying to do all along was to photograph desire, that oftentimes dark force that moves and shapes our existence. CGC

The poems that travel in this realm are extraordinary. Desire moves between the opposite poles of objectification and subjectification. Its correlatives are sex, addiction, obsession, devotion, manipulation, and ultimately death. This poetry is powerful because it taps this dark energy and brings it to the light of day, to the lips of the poet. Consider the dark clarity of "foto 1" and the gaze that it freezes:

> un filtro pretende obfuscar
> las emociones del mundo
> mientras tú repites en tonos grises
> el juego con las muñecas en la cama
>
> claude monet's waterlilies
> are splattered about in books
> but the erotic colors can't touch you
>
> tan cerca de ti
> que pudiera acariciar tus pechos
>
> sigo tratando de entender la técnica
> the particular exposure
> of your shattered past
> y la manera obsesiva
> con que manipulas las muñecas
>
> that's always been your problem
> dices enfadada
> you can't feel things
> cause you're too busy
> trying to understand them
>
> you used to like that about me
>
> pues ya no . . .

Fotos (1993): 3

The diction and register are as fresh and colloquial as they are profound and insightful. English and Spanish flow freely into one another in an extraordinary synthesis and synergy. "Foto 9" is a study in black on black:

> negro que se teje en negro

las palabras fácilmente pueden ser
un remolino de cuchillos

es difícil penetrar superficies cuadradas
donde ni siquiera existen sombras
pero sé que estás allí
derrotada
tatuaje en tus pechos
tu mirada ahogada en alcohol . . .

in the total darkness there's a river
with the black waters of fate
slowly maneuvering to consciousness
fragments of illusions . . .

Fotos (1993): 25-26

The dreamlike images then dissolve into a raucous, no-win lovers'
argument, after which the only solace is a solitary walk on a dark
street. The last photograph is of an armed stand-off between deranged
lovers in a leafless cottonwood forest:

. . . the choice is yours
i say extending my arm
to the four directions of the world

you sonofabitch

te seguiré amando

I'll kill you

nunca te olvidaré

in a moment
the quivering blackness of the shadows
will swallow the winter sun

two fat shreds of clouds roll around
in the monstrous blue silence

the insistent reflection
dances off the gun

and as i walk on
accepting the inevitability of fear
three blue jays swoop
in front of me
and take my breath away

i could photograph them forever
gliding around a glistening gun barrel
around dancing shadows
around a selfdoubting philosopher
an insecure pervert
and my demon-infested amada

yes the one who betrays me
la que maldice mi ser
la que me inspira eternamente

Fotos (1993): 28-31

The muse may become disfigured and traitorous, but in the end she is still the muse.

In his most recent collection, García-Camarillo returns to the automatic symbolic language and integrative power of dreams:

[*Dream-Walking* (1994) — cover notes]

Dreams taste like the purest form of metaphor. To dream is to walk a journey of renewal where the oppressive, rational censor in all of us is irrelevant. *Dream-Walking* es una colección de 14 bilingual poems I originally recorded in my journal as the remembered dreams de un período muy intenso y controversial en mi vida. Me fascinan los sueños because I have absolutely no control over their content. Me molesta no haber desarrollado la capacidad para entenderlos profundamente, ya que reconozco que por medio de ese chaos of illogical symbols we share with ourselves información para comprender la complejidad que somos. Sospecho que siempre conservaré la necesidad de tejer imágenes soñadas in the texture of my poems. I need this liberating movida que nomás no puedo encontrar anywhere else. CGC

In one of the most healing dream sequences, dream "4," the poet returns at different ages to various scenes with his parents, including his father's deathbed. This poem is cited near the beginning of this text. In dream "6," with his father in a burning house with horses running through it, the poet finally sees the route of his deliverance:

> . . . what can I do
> with the pain papá
> do you have any suggestions
>
> the house and the horses
> burn furiously
>
> i know i won't finish the letter
> before everything turns to ashes
>
> and i try to understand
> why the bedroom window
> por donde entra
> y sale mi mundo
> hasn't burned
>
> it hangs there
> surrounded by fire
>
> i wonder what kept me
> from seeing it before

Dream-Walking (1994): 17-18

There are dreams of pursuit, violence, and death in this collection. Oneiric imagery has always been a part of the poetry of García-Camarillo, but in earlier phases of his work it often lacked the extraordinary resonance and narrative control present here. Although he claims in his prefatory notes that he wishes he could interpret his dreams better, his dream-poems are masterfully rendered, saturated with symbol, significance, and feeling. A sense of integrated equilibrium is the sign of this master dreamer and weaver of visions.

Dream-Walking is a psychotropic catalog of wishes, fears, obsessions, and desires. The entire expressive range of the poet's social and interior poetic universe is contained herein. In yet another *ars poética*, dream "7," the poet contemplates the source of his song and reaffirms his commitment to sing it:

they hurl river rocks
and curse like maniacs
as they tighten the circle

the power of the word is mine
and you'll have to kill me
cause i won't give it back
she whispers

until she finally collapses
on a puddle of blood

i drive myself to a hospital
in my old vw van

the head wounds
are especially painful
and i can't see with one eye

but it doesn't matter
cause i'm listening to the voice
that can't be bought or stolen
but must be earned
with a clarity of mind
and patience

there's a mound of rocks
by the river
that sings

i have nothing
but the words
to tell my story
are you ready
for the words
are you ready
for my words

the bleeding woman is dying
as she murmurs the song

that is a fluttering leaf
in my ear

aha there's the curve
and jammed against the woods
the hospital

i can hardly think now
but i understand

and i will sing
till the end of my days
i promise

Dream-Walking (1994): 19-20

Cecilio García-Camarillo has been singing for a quarter of a century. Many lesser poets have seized the center stage of celebrity and been praised. Fewer have worked through as much and experimented as much with as much persistence as this Tejano. Although relatively few critics and readers have heard his song, when they do the realization will become clear that this poet has one of the most evolved and expressive voices in the broadening range of Chicano literature.

E. R. L.
April, 2000

References

Alurista, "Introduction," in Cecilio García-Camarillo, Carmen Tafolla, and Reyes Cárdenas, *Get Your Tortillas Together* (San Antonio, Texas: Cultural Distribution Center, 1976).

Evangelina Vigil, "Una mordida de *Get Your Tortillas Together*, poesía de Cecilio García-Camarillo, Reyes Cárdenas, and Carmen Tafolla (an analytic poem)," *Caracol*, 3, 9 (May 1977): 17.

Max Martínez, "Los Mejores Escritores de Aztlán," *Rayas*, 2 (March-April 1978): 3.

Max Martínez, "Max-y-más," *Carta Abierta*, 15 (Summer 1979): 8-9.

Salvador Rodríguez del Pino, "La poesía chicana: una nueva trayectoria," in *The Identification and Analysis of Chicano Literature*, Francisco Jiménez, ed. (New York: Bilingual Press/Editorial Bilingüe, 1979): 68-89.

Carlos Nicolás Flores, "A Tribute to Cecilio García Camarillo," *Revista Río Bravo: En Honor de Cecilio García Camarillo, Chicano Poet, Editor, Activist, Hijo de Laredo*, 1, 1 (Winter 1981): 17, 19.

Cecilio García-Camarillo, "Poesía Chicana," *Revista Río Bravo: En Honor de Cecilio García Camarillo, Chicano Poet, Editor, Activist, Hijo de Laredo*, 1, 1 (Winter 1981): 7.

Catalina Reyes, "Play Gives Comic Twist to Virgin Appearance," *Albuquerque Journal*, December 19, 1992.

Cecilio García-Camarillo, "Interview with Enrique R. Lamadrid," February 27, 1995, Albuquerque, New Mexico, Special Collections, Zimmerman Library University of New Mexico.

Papers

García-Camarillo's papers are held in the Special Collections Department of the Zimmerman Library, University of New Mexico, Albuquerque.

Bibliography

Chapbooks

Get Your Tortillas Together (with Carmen Tafolla and Reyes Cárdenas). San Antonio, Texas: Cultural Distribution Center, 1976.
Hang a Snake. Albuquerque: Mano Izquierda Books, 1981.
Ecstasy and Puro Pedo. Albuquerque: Mano Izquierda Books, 1981.
Winter Month. Albuquerque: Mano Izquierda Books, 1982.
Calcetines Embotellados. Albuquerque: Mano Izquierda Books, 1982.
Carambola. Albuquerque: Mano Izquierda Books, 1982.
Double-Face. Albuquerque: Mano Izquierda Books, 1982.
Cuervos en el Río Grande. Albuquerque: Mano Izquierda Books, 1983.
Burning Snow. Albuquerque: Mano Izquierda Books, 1984.
Borlotes Mestizos. Albuquerque: Mano Izquierda Books, 1984.
The Line. Albuquerque: Mano Izquierda Books, 1984.
Soy pajarita. Albuquerque: Mano Izquierda Books, 1986.
Black Horse on the Hill. Albuquerque: Mano Izquierda Books, 1988.
Zafa'o. Albuquerque: Mano Izquierda Books, 1992.
Crickets. Albuquerque: Mano Izquierda Books, 1992.
Fotos. Albuquerque: Mano Izquierda Books, 1993.
Dream-Walking. Albuquerque: Mano Izquierda Books, 1994.
Tlalli. Albuquerque: Mano Izquierda Books, 2000.

Other

"Noche de Aquellas," in Arnold C. Vento, Alurista, José Peregrino Flores, eds., *Flor y Canto II: An Anthology of Chicano Literature* (Albuquerque and San Antonio: Pajarito Publications and University of Texas-Austin Center for Mexican-American Studies, 1975): 67.
"Cartero," "A La Edad de 35 Años," "Quetzalcoatl," "Mujer / Quetzalcoatl," "Ojo," "Por Tus Ojos," and "Suroeste," in *El Quetzal Emplumece* (San Antonio: Mexican American Cultural Center, 1976): 103-107.
"un bato con las manos abiertas," (poema concreto), in Alurista, ed., *Trece Aliens* (San Diego: University of California, 1976): cover.
"Periquiando en Aztlán," in *Dale Gas: Chicano Art of Texas: An Exhibition of Contemporary Chicano Art* (Houston: Contemporary Arts Museum, 1977): 7.
"The Lake" and "Las 4 direcciones del mundo y el centro," in *Canto al Pueblo: An Anthology of Experiences* (San Antonio: Penca Books, 1978): 22-25.

Gabriel García Márquez, "The Woman Who Came in at Six," trans. Cecilio García-Camarillo, in José Armas, ed., *Mestizo: An Anthology of Chicano Literature* (Albuquerque: Pajarito Publications, 1978): 99-108.

"tejiendo," in Rudolfo A. Anaya and Simon J. Ortiz, eds., *Ceremony of Brotherhood* (Albuquerque: Academia Publications, 1981): 92.

"el ex-pinto todo contento," "el chavo de west tejas," "sapos," and in *Revista Río Bravo: En Honor de Cecilio García Camarillo, Chicano Poet, Editor, Activist, Hijo de Laredo* 1, 1 (Winter 1981): 6.

"Víbora Energía" and "Hombre Mariposa," poems by García-Camarillo with Itzolín V. García in *Resiembra* (Española, New Mexico: Conjunto Cultural Norteño, 1982): 42-43.

"Juvencio," "rancho," "compassionate heart," and "chivo," in Nicolás Kanellos, ed., *A Decade of Hispanic Literature: An Anniversary Anthology, Revista Chicano-Riqueña* 10, 1-2 (invierno-primavera 1982): 73-76.

"Portrait," "hormigas," and "eagle," in *And the Ground Spoke . . .* with Joy Harjo, E. A. Mares and Jim Sagel, (San Antonio: The Guadalupe Cultural Center, 1986): 5-14.

"El ex-pinto todo contento," in Rudolfo A. Anaya, ed., *Voces: An Anthology of Nuevo Mexicano Writers* (Albuquerque: El Norte Publications, 1987): 117-120.

"Le bouc (Chivo)," "Origines (Orígenes)," "Album de famille (Family photographs)," "Cloture ancestrale (Ancestral fence)," "Retour (Going home)," in Elyette Benjamin-Labarthe, ed. and trans., *Vous avez dit Chicano: anthologie thématique de poésie chicano,* (Bordeaux: Editions de la Maison des Sciences de l'Homme d'Aquitaine, 1993): 128-9, 196-9, 202-5.

"Peculiar Smile," in Jeanie C. Williams and Victor de Suvero, eds., *Saludos!: Poemas de Nuevo México* (Tesuque, N. M.: Pennywhistle, 1995): 106-107.

Selected Periodical Publications—Uncollected

"cuentista," "espíritu," "el embrujo del frijol," "correr," "página," "abuelo," "mano," "dientes de la noche," "crimen," "calles," "fingersliquid," "cabeza," "domingo," "haikus," and poemas concretos: "lluvia marxista," "frío," "winter," "hormiguero," "aire triste," "naturaleza es cadáver," *El Grito—La Voz Poética del Chicano,* 7, 3 (March-May 1974): 29-45.

"Alma," *Maize: Cuaderno de Arte y Literatura Xicana,* 1, 2 (winter 1977): 14-15.

"y la cólera aplastante . . . ," "viendo un lago," "nopal y piedras," "silenciosa," "medianoche" (poemas concretos), *Maize: Cuaderno de Arte y Literatura Xicana*, 1, 4 (verano 1978): 39-42.

"Juvencio," "rancho," "compassionate heart," "chivo," *Revista Chicano-Riqueña* (Los Tejanos), 8, 3 (verano 1980): 36-39.

"Calcetines Embotellados," *Huehuetitlán*, 9 (Diciembre 1988): 16.

"peculiar smile," *Blue Mesa Review*, 3 (1991): 57.

"Rectángulos Carcomidos: Es Absurda, the Consuming Power of Guilt; Sonriendo Me Dices que con Besos You'll Drive Away My Evil Thoughts; Dudo Seriamente the Goodness of the Heart; El Nuevo Deseo de Odiar Es tan Viejo; Huir Otra Vez del Contacto Humano" (poemas concretos), *Puerto del Sol* (Special Supplement: Caló), 27, 1 (1992): 111-116.

Editorial Work and Cultural Journalism

Magazín. San Antonio, 1971-72.

"Poesía: un anti-essay," *Magazín*, 1, 2 (November 1971): 42.

El Quetzal Emplumece, edited by Cecilio García-Camarillo with Carmela Montalvo, and Leonardo Anguiano (San Antonio: Mexican American Cultural Center, 1976).

Caracol. San Antonio, 1974-77: 80.

Nahualliandoing: Poetry in Español/Nahuatl/English, editor, introductory notes (San Antonio: Caracol, 1977).

Rayas. Albuquerque, 1978-79.

"Writing that Poem for a Chicano Magazine," *Rayas*, 5 (September-October 1978): 3.

Flow of the River, script for video with Miguel A. Gandert and Sabine R. Ulibarrí (Albuquerque: Hispanic Culture Foundation, 1988).

"Espejos de Aztlán" Chicano cultural affairs program. KUNM, Albuquerque 1979—present.

Interviews include Rudy Anaya, Ricardo Sánchez, José Montalvo, Estevan Arellano, Tomás Atencio escritores mexicanos, art, politics, drug addicts, prisoners, midwives, social-action Cubans right and left, Chile, Guatemala, Nicaragua, El Salvador—not-for-profit groups involved in social change and the arts, *homenaje a* Cleofas Vigil, Reies López Tijerina, and so forth.

Play Adaptations and Productions

Vista del Puente (*A View From the Bridge* by Arthur Miller), La Compañía de Teatro de Albuquerque, November 1, December 4, 1983.

Tartuffe Tafoya (*Tartuffe* by Moliere), La Compañía de Teatro de Albuquerque, May 17-June 30, 1985.

Puente Negro (by Estela Portillo Trambley), La Compañía de Teatro de Albuquerque, Winter 1985.

Spanish Fly (*Mandragola*, by Niccolo Machiavelli), La Compañía de Teatro de Albuquerque, March 17-May 7, 1989.

Bienvenido, Don Goyito (by Manuel Méndez Ballester), La Compañía de Teatro de Albuquerque, June 14-24, 1990.

La Virgen del Tepeyac (original play), La Compañía de Teatro de Albuquerque, December 11-20, 1992.

A Chicano Christmas Carol (from *A Christmas Carol* by Charles Dickens), La Compañía de Teatro de Albuquerque, December 19-22, 1991, and December 1-11, 1994.

para Domi

rancho

a qué le tiras
crouching todo el día
on this sandpapered land
of malnutritioned shrubs

la luna
parece una tuerca
de plastic

my soul
well
there's plastic in it too

city acid has galloped
through veins
and you've let a few books
curdle your mind cells

y 'ora la onda sarcástica
de pito descontrolado
is that life's
a many-colored mexican bag
fattened by engusanado days

it's more
ese
just wait

your beard's still growing

family photographs

heat
rots your breath

a sagging stench
all around

feel like
unhooking carátula
and feeding it to
las vacas de plomo

shriveled family photographs
melting time
y busco por acá y allá
with desperate microscopic eyes

only ants
and horned toads
move about

the farm
is a melting
giant ribcage

your lips
rip open
as you giggle

and the tentáculos
del sol
lash about
through cracks

chivo

egg-yoke
colored morning

and tongue hangs like a scar

these last 3 nights
your snake eyes
have seen the wind
snarl like a prophet
with a cancerous stomach

it's then i see
el chivo con olor de azufre

he first circles me
darting up
flopping down

tightening
and like a black bubble
he starts floating

tighter
soot-black his jerky sulphur breath
gagging me

driving his face
into yours

and now you know he looks like me
like you felt it all along

you recoil

like an old hingeless barn door
you collapse

vecino

dice que she rode
rat-tailed days
with her
penny's worth of life

a miserable
wheelbarrowful of wrinkles

pero terca
managing to hang-on
ghost-pale
her eyes slopping sewers

dice que
he could see
death's hairy hands
clutching her throat

pero terca
white as bone
terca como ponzoña de víbora
she hung on

i swear i loved my mother
pero chingao
nomás ya no pude
and i groaned
goddamn god
take her out of my sight
or i'll run the fucking tractor over her
do you hear

that happened a pile of years ago
on the 20th of this month i'll be 80

compassionate heart

you jerk around
the days
like a headless rooster

pendejo

crees que eres
a screwy poet

when are you stopping
the rattlings in your head

the stars
are stars
no granos de sal
tossed on your fate

cut the crap
your heart will tick
for only so long

hug that as a fact

open up
your compassionate heart

stop toying
around with the ego

don't try to get
a ridiculous jump
on death

to ecstasy
y puro pedo

i commit
the senses

i criminal
water the words
then bleed the words

water the sun
then erase the sun

i
& xerox copy of myself

hummingbird baila
en árbol de la vida

hummingbird
picotea
2 canciones
2 arcoirises
de la máscara

flag of duality
snakes in my heart

snake
hides in the void
of the heart

el cielo
tiene un agujero

void
of the land

el cielo
esconde su agujero
del olvido

hummingbird
pierces the void
of the eyes

how one wakes up
is as important as
running into a rattlesnake

it's hard to type together all the edges of my identity
in gringo-america
exactly 12 noon

i pull an old coffin up the hill by the creek
in my poetry
images must move

death on a country path
is brief
not so depression

11/1970

no sé cómo empecé a arreglar
cajones rotos espejos
sillas del cuarto apagado
o de algún sueño diabólico
ruidos llantos visiones
como carcajadas rojas
como sangre espesa arrumbada
formando mi cara
en abstracciones que sólo los fines
de la conciencia conocen
no sé por qué escarbo como maníaco en el pasado
como máquina eléctrica
sacando libras sobre libras
de ponzoña muerta
de repente existen sólo 4 paredes
un diccionario
y yo
pero yo no soy yo
y no sé en dónde estoy

el aire está encebollado es espeso
trato de definirme
pero aparecen fotografías son cadáveres
con pantalones de alambres eléctricos
y sombreros de gotas de saliva
los cigarros no parpadean
son payasos los minutos
he asesinado al color verde
cada palabra termina en frustración
la cabeza es una máquina de escribir llena de ácido
el colchón tiene sal y uvas podridas
es inútil
las bisagras de las puertas no hablan
hace frío bajo el pellejo plástico

se siente podrido el viento
en el círculo vicioso de la definición

qué es la diferencia entre la fotografía
y el cadáver

entonces traía el sombrero blanco con la banda roja
y sunglasses
pa' enfrentármele de aquellas al summer
del southwest

fumaba aunque me hacía daño el humo y los minutos
eran payasos europeos

me gustaba el color verde porque estaba seguro
que era la piel de la frustración

los huesos de la mano
acarician la máquina de escribir
pero no suelta sentimientos

cómo jode el rechinido de las bisagras de la puerta
hace frío
bajo este pellejo plástico

un animal
se traga la pintura
roja del silencio

la onda es de encuerar
los sentimientos
y escribirlos

pero se engarruñan los dedos
ante la inmensidad de la página

la pluma
es un cucaracho pataleando

si quemo el pilar
que sostiene el resorte
de la noche
se cae la luna como un cuchillo

flotan en un río
automóviles podridos
como microbios
en una llaga

la mente es un foco rojo
calentando las piernas de una mujer

el cielo con su interminable lluvia gris
bombas depresivas
punzadas
y el constante deseo de no ser
deseo de parar de una patada
las alas del reloj
parar el sonido
de martillo enterrando clavos en los huesos
las palabras son cadáveres
que caen por los dientes
pero diez dedos pálidos
solamente peinan el pelo
como líquidos muertos
como esponjas desaguadas
quizás mañana también esté lloviendo
y quiera cortar los hilos tan enterrados
que me amarran contra paredes
lluvia gris caes como el vómito
de una vida muy enferma

hago el cuerpo desnudo
una cruz
y lo pongo en la loma
pa' que el sol lo haga lumbre
y luego las cenizas rueden a fertilizar
mi raíz en el barrio
me sentaba en rincones
navajeando
silencios
queriendo oír la música oscura
de la carne
descifrando
la infinita confusión de la imaginación
amachada
en ciertas palabras anímicas

hoy en este bello otoño
veo con ojos destapados
a 4 chotas destruirle la cabeza
a un chavalón

escupo
con nervioso coraje
las hojas secas

y siento
el viento fresco e introvertido
estrujarme
los testículos

aunque
telaraña
del tiempo
quiere amarrar espíritu

digo secretos
y acaricio
ojos de vena'o

pa' poder
serruchar
lo importante
del hervidero de contradicciones

tejido
a mi compañera

azadoniamos
plantamos
regamos

ombligo
de aztlán

pa' poder
cosechar ideales

Canción

camina en sí
camina en sí

porque no tiene patria
                presidente
                iglesia
                o dinero

camina en sí
camina en sí

con 122 libras de conciencia
                contra la guerra
                    de los gringos
                      en vietnam

camina en sí
camina en sí

porque es chicano
        de aztlán
                y habla caló

camina en sí
camina en sí

        sin amar
          o ser amado
                en el egoísmo
        de blue jeans
            barba
              bigote
y greña que cuelga hasta la cintura

camina en sí

camina en sí

cargando
    las gruesas contradicciones
      de chavo colonizado
        en su huelga de hambre

camina en sí
camina en sí

    escupe
        ríe
    y en la chaveta
      vuelve a 'cariciar
con dedos de vapor
      un jarro de frijoles

camina en sí
camina en sí

firme en su bronca
    poco jorobado
        los ojos hundiéndose
           hastas los orígenes
    y sobando el anillo
        plateado de la muerte

camina en sí
camina en sí

           1971

Juvencio

cuando ella voltió
   la esquina
      rechinando
      los dientes
y tartamudiando
       —viejo baboso—
   juvencio
     sintió
que se le remachó
en el corazón
    una cruz
      filuda
        de donde colgaban
      unos calzones rojos
        con nalgas jugosas

en la cheveta
     se desató
       un atajo
       de remolinos
       y el zumbido
       en las orejas
   hacía a juvencio
     sentirse zurumbato
       pero
       pos yesca
    la mano
      tembloriza
   se sambutió
      en los chones
        con nalga
después del chingazo
      se sintió
       sofocado
como que lo habían
      tapao

con piedras

cuando
   esnapió
      se bambalió
         pa la iglesia

      y juvencio
rezó
y rezó
      mientras la lengua
        de su mente
           barría los subterráneos
              de una seda
                 roja
      y perfumada

1974

Tarde y patas

tarde esqueletuda

    tierruda
    enfermuda
    putuda
    pobresuda
    mugresuda
    lagrimuda
    colonizuda

patas con callos

    con cansancio
    con silencio
    con hambre
    con tristeza
    con dolor
    con carabinas
    con revolución

1975

Árbol de naranjas

mi raíz
    honda
        rasca
                el ombligo
                del planeta

dicen
    que le pertenezco
        a un gringo político
        del valle de tejas

pero los únicos
    que conozco
        son los chicanos

        que me dan agua
que se sientan en mi sombra
que me dicen chistes
que me acarician

paque no me enoje
        cuando me arrancan
           mis hijos

año tras año
    con mi fruta
        continúa la vida

porque mi raíz
    es tan honda
        como dios

1976

Preparándonos pa' la marcha
de Muleshoe a Austin, Tejas 1.27

                    pasan por mi mente mil poemas
en un instante
            porque se necesita tanta fuerza
                    para captar las acciones
                            de mi gente
don claudio
        desdoblando
            las banderas rojas

luis rascándole la costilla
        a la guitarra
                que suelta
                una palomita triste

        las señoras en la cocina
                cocinando
                            la energía
que nos llevará por el frío

moya tomando fotografías
            para conjelar
            para siempre
                    pedazos de esta mañana
                            en muleshoe, tejas

                david
barriendo el coraje
                        y determinación
            del piso de cemento
                    donde todos dormimos anoche
la señora salas
        firme y pensativa
            madre de la unión de campesinos
                de tejas
                    toma café y le reza
a la madre de toda la raza

la sagrada virgen de guadalupe

                todos esperamos
                con la impaciencia
                de potros encorralados

la llegada del arzobispo de lubbock
        que por fin nunca llegó
                a ofrecernos misa
(porque según el mensaje del bato
        estaba demasiado frío)

                pos qué pedo
                    ay se va
                porque ya todos sabemos
que nuestro verdadero trabajo
        es caminar los caminos
                en nuestra lucha eterna
                de buscar justicia
                en nuestra marcha eterna
de echarle en cara
                    y gritarle
        al gringo capitalista
            ya basta
            ya basta
con la explotación de los pobres

                                1979

the cat
frowns at the snow
endlessly

eating the salad
but your eyes
are so blue so blue

you're so peaceful
talking of going away
once again

so you cut your hair
to please yourself
and displease me

⁂

the crows & i
pace up & down
the river we like so much

⁂

all of a sudden
much of my hair is white
amazing

the intense blue
of the jay
burns into the snow

whatever it is
those snow tracks
look scary

yes
death
is like a field full of snow

The Line

para Teresa

1.

6 am
and i drink a cup of hot tea
i got from john lansa of old oraibi
that puts some magic in my body
then head out
for the food stamp line

freezing out here
i spit
and the whole thing
turns into a greenish chunk of ice

walk about two blocks
and it starts snowing
and i say with my whole gut
oh shit
but it only lasts a few minutes

2.

at the food stamp parking lot
and this scrubby gabacho
in a toyota pickup
tries to pick up two incredible
food stamp chicks
wearing only light sweaters

and they cuss him out loud
so everybody can hear
goddamn macho asshole
this is the south valley
and it ain't the place
for that kind of shit

and we all laugh
the horny guy out of existence
with our half frozen faces

3.

the old regulars
at the food stamp line
about 25 of the early-rising warriors

and we wait it out
and wait
and before we know it
it gets even colder than hell
and there's about 100 of us
waiting and waiting
and the snot on our noses turns to ice

4.

the security guard goes by
an affalable looking lady
blonde with wild matted hair
with a perpetual ironic smile
and a sort of goose walk

but everybody grimly eyeballs her
from head to toe
cuz to us she's the enemy
who gives the orders and bosses the line
and besides
where the fuck does she hide with her gun
when the riots happen

5.

a 60 year old pachuco
with greased hair combed back
and centipede-looking scar on his forehead
offers a 2 year old giggly girl some candy

but the mother
with the nicest smile
says no sir
it's just too early for that garbage

6.

the sky
turns into a chunk of ice

we do shuffling dances
to keep our blood
from freezing

7.

a neighborhood drunk who's about 35
but looks 50
staggers up the line
to a ghostly old grey man
with a jimmy durante nose
who is reading a newspaper

he taps the grey ghost
on the back and quickly squats

the ghost
turns and smiles at the fat lady behind him
who's squeezing to death a big purse
against her breasts

as soon as the old ghost
turns back to his newspaper
the drunk again taps him on the shoulder

again the grey ghost
turns and smiles
at the elephant lady
who's getting pissed and yells at him
it's not me it's that goddamn fool

the drunk jumps up with a barrage
of wine-laughter and the ghost
smiles and shakes his hand

the crowd joins in the joke
with belly laughs
that keep us from freezing

8.

at around 8
the social worker hacks
file in
looking straight ahead
with cadaverous eyes
and double chins propped against their chests

and the gossip picks up
scums
you'd think it was their stamps
they sit on their fat asses all day
they don't give a damn about our starving
their fucking salaries are our tax money
they'd be dead by now if they were out here
they're the ones causing the riots
they got food look at em they're all fat
i'd like to beat the living hell out of that one's
ugly face

9.

i look around and check
the poor faces of my people waiting it out
chicanos whites a few blacks and indians

all with the hard core evidence
of flesh and minds
that have been on the front lines
of life's daily battles

we're all poor
and we're all freezing out here
and we're all talking
and laughing
with the electricity
that only the underdogs possess

10.

a young chick
in tight jeans
with a body getting soft
and blowing out
talks about her abortions

another in a light sweater
is already turning purple from the cold
she shivers like a maniac
and talks to the crowd about her husband
and his brother
having a fist-fight over the weekend

a short old lady with an eagle nose
surrounded by wrinkles talks about the riot
of last week and how she almost got trampled
and how nobody gives a damn about the old

11.

the security guard with matted hair
walks up and down the line
she opens her freezing mouth wide
and shouts into the crowd
that today is blue card day
and everyone must have a blue card

and for a minute
the sun breaks through the grey ice
over the sandías
o man
how utterly nice
a ripple of solidarity loosens up and down
our strangely formed line
we take deep breaths
into our half-frozen lungs

and then it's over
and the smiling guard
shouts again
it's blue card day
only blue cards

12.

a tiny old lady
with a baby-girl's face
standing like a slab of ice in front of me
suddenly giggles
and says she's got a blue card

her grand-daughter michelle saiz
who's waiting in the car
just told her
i'm the nurse at armijo school

i tell her i'm just the health aide
and even though i work full time
the salary is so bad
i have to get food stamps to make it

yes the country seems to be rotting away
and she's scared of more rioting
and she wishes the old folks and cripples
could go in first to get the stamps

sure that seems pretty fair
but a hunched over tall middle-class type lady
that's behind me
snarls loudly that everybody has to wait on the line

everybody has to wait it out
we're all equals here
she shrieks foaming at the mouth
then she starts coughing
spitting and coughing
then she turns blue and almost folds over
coughs lots more
then stumbles away from the line

13.

michelle skips over

she's a 4th grader with kinky hair
cute mestizo face
and we talk about the heavy snow we just had
about cartoons
about the bossy new principal at armijo school
who wears tons of make-up
and about michelle's pretending to be sick
so she can stay out of school
like today

i tell her that when teachers get boring
she should say she has a headache
and come and stay with me at the nurse's office
lots of kids do that

14.

the line starts moving
there are several hundred of us now
but we're close to the door
and we don't give a damn
cuz we won't have to wait much longer

and we jump like chickens
talking and laughing
to keep from freezing onto the concrete

the security guard with the matted hair
is still smiling
and finally she herds my group
into the building

ahhhhh
it's so great to sit for a while
in this pigsty of a hallway that's so warm
damn it's almost ecstatic

15.

i kid michelle
about her hair turning red
and she smiles at me

her little-girl faced grandmother
insists on talking about armijo school

do i really like the job
not really the teachers are snobbish
and very uptight
and the pay is lousy
but the kids are great

well all her children went to armijo
and now her grandchildren
she knows some of the teachers through michelle
there are so many discipline problems
at schools these days

i tell her about the new principal
that dyes her hair black
and has siamese cat eyes
and wears pounds of lipstick

well she's pretty good about keeping the school
clean and in order

well for sure she's got to meet
this new strange principal
and in her book if the principal keeps everybody
in order she can continue being strange

16.

but we can't talk now

the group is called again
and in a sort of icy daze we wait some more
in this big stuffy totally empty room
that i immediately associate with
concentration camps

but anyway
i join the crowd in smiling hotly
with the smell of victory
just behind the big glass window

they call us again
and i get $173 for the month

i take a deep breath
and head home
through the lines of my people
still waiting it out
shoving
cussing
laughing
joking
refusing to surrender to the deadly cold
in this our daily struggle for survival

Ojos de rata

1.

sabes que'l bato
tenía ojos de rata

ni más
ni menos
así nació

ojos chiquitos
ojos chiquitos y redondos
ojos chiquitos y redondos y relumbrosos
ojos chiquitos y redondos y relumbrosos y fríos

2.

no sé
pero chanza
que por eso lo mataron
los perros
esa noche
ese sábado por la noche
que había estao
con su novia
en el dairy queen
por la isleta

risa y risa
comiendo nieve
y risa y risa
and joke after joke
cuz the guy
had a sense of humor
that would make a gringo tv comedy
look like a funeral procession

3.

and at around 11 pm
he took her home
and before she opened the door
of his hung-down 70 chevy
he told her
that he really dug
being with her
cuz he felt so complete
me entiendes cómo honey
me haces sentir
como que valgo la pena
de ser hombre
and it's you
being the way you are
and your laughing
that make me feel this way

and she kissed him
and said
call me soon and don't you forget it

4.

el ojos de rata
cranked up the ranfla
tuned his radio to kabq
and sings along to a rola
by little joe y la familia
esa que dice algo de que todos
traemos la virgen de guadalupe
en el pecho

órale pues
el ojos de rata
is feeling real good

5.

he cruises on isleta to the north
and turns west on lovato
that little street 'onde 'stá
jay's plumbing
pulling it all together
then he swings around saavedra
to bridge
rumbo pa' atrisco

el ojos de rata
nunca esperaba que
de aquel ladito de 5 points
lo comenzará a seguir
una carrucha de perros

ay vienen los perros
cuídate ojos de rata
te siguen los perros
traen hambre los perros

6.

pero cuando le puso
pa'l south en atrisco
heading pa arenal
el ojos de rata
todavía no sentía
a los 2 perros
hovering behind the victim

de volada lo pararon
y chanza que cuando le hecharon
la luz del flashlight
en los ojos
al ojos de rata

the animal instinct de los perros
was confirmed to the max

right on
aquí 'stá the perfect
saturday night south valley greaser
those eyes
tell us he's up to no good
chinga'o qué ojos tan feos
parece que te los regaló el diablo cabrón

7.

cuidao ojos de rata
te quieren chingar
las bestias with a badge on

pero el ojos de rata
nomás se ríe
and did as he was told

el chavo got out of his heavy chevy
and put his head and arms on the hood
he spread his legs wide
and even when the flashlight
was pushed hard against his neck
el ojos de rata no se quejó ni nada

pero cuando he felt
que uno de los perros
comenzó a 'garrarle las nalgas
el ojos de rata   .
gritó hey man
what the hell's going on
what the hell
you think you're doin'

and that's all the perros
wanted to hear
to ravage their prey

truchas ojos de rata
cuidao camarada ojos de rata

pero de volada
le cayeron los flashlights
en la cabeza pescuezo espalda
y todo lugar

y cuando cayó el ojos de rata
boca arriba he cracked his skull
on a stone
and he never woke up

8.

el ojos de rata
cerró los ojos
and went into a coma
and never opened his rat eyes
nunca más
pobre chavo
i wonder si cuando estabas
medio muerto
te preguntaste
pos que chingaos hice yo

and you never
figured it out
y te enterraron
y moriste
por la simple razón
que naciste chicano colonizado
en una nación imperialista
pudriéndose en sus enfermedades

de clase
dinero
y racismo

los perros are free
roaming around the south valley
looking for more bros como tú

la chavala finally got married
con un bato that you used to beat at pool
all the time

y el ojos de rata
pos no sé
y cómo va a saber uno de esas cosas

pero como el ojos de rata
era católico aunque nunca iba a misa
pos chanza que dios wachó
todo la injusticia
de esa noche

y chanza que el ojos de rata
hoy mismo 'ta descansando en el cielo

El ex-pinto todo contento

wáchalo
here he comes
todo contento
con una sonrisa de oreja a oreja
que parece una rebanada de sandía

viene todo contento
wáchalo
con su chuco walk
los brazos swinging in rhythm
to a subconscious polka

here he comes
wáchalo
por la isleta en el southwest valley
en su barrio
vacilando in his cosmology
y tirándole good vibes
a las barrio queens
with indian faces
and tight jeans
that cruise by

mira
wáchale
los tattoos de aquellas que trai el bato
en el brazo derecho
en technicolor y toda la cosa
trai a la virgen de guadalupe
y en el izquierdo
a la fregada
wáchale
pero cúrate bien

el ex-pinto trai a la gran huesuda
la muerte que se wachea
bien proud and defiant
and she's holding una víbora de bastón

y te das cuenta
que los tattoos
pos they're covering
the needle tracks of the wasteland
where he lost his self-respect
me entiendes cómo

and the purple scar that's shaped
like a new moon
allí detrás de la oreja izquierda
pos allí fue donde le descargó
el flashlight
that fatal night
an overanxious rookie cop

y de allí lo descontaron pa la pinta
wounded y todo el pedo
pero ay viene ahora wáchalo
todo contento
sporting an emiliano zapata bigote
above the never-ending chorro
of good-hearted carcajadas

nació en el barrio
sufrió en el barrio
torció en el barrio
y aquí viene otra vez
wáchalo
todo contento

pero cúrate cómo mira
wáchale como usa los ojos
simón que sí
ay está la movida y transformación
el bato mira con ojos concientizados
porque en la pinta
se le prendió el foco
como hombrecito sin miedo
se agarró a chingazos con la realidad
de su vida
y plasticó con prisioneros políticos
y leyó del movimiento chicano
y el camarada snapped forever

y ora ay viene
wáchalo
todo contento
por la isleta
saludando pacá y payá
feeling the sun darkening his skin

he kicks a beer can
a few times
with his mexican guaraches
y se ríe con ojos concientizados

wáchalo
ta en su barrio
donde hay que vivir y jalar

wáchalo cómo ahora trai hambre
so he goes into a restaurant
and sits by the window
and orders menudo

wáchalo
cómo mira pa' fuera
scanning his barrio que conoce tan bien
knowing onde stá el desmadre
y la fantasía loca
wáchale
como mira el mundo

'tá todo contento
el ex-pinto
'tá todo contento
por estar libre con ojos concientizados

El chavo de West Tejas

1.

me arremango
las mangas de la camisa
le doy una patada
a la puerta
y entro al "sírvanme otra bar"

de volada saludo a la mary
la morena chaparrita de pelo largo color de noche
la siempre riendo chicanita de pechos jugosos
y le pido
una falsa por favor

siento los brazos
como si fueran de plomo
siento como que me pasó una troca
por la espalda

todo el chingao santo día en el sol
y sale uno como que trai rabia

no tanto del miserable sol
sino rabia
desta pinche vida que va de peor en peor

pero aquí no hay jefe gringo
mayugándome el pulmón
aquí yo puedo ser yo

2.

pa' alivianarme
meto la mano en la bolsa
saco una peseta
y le pongo patrás del cuarto

pa' dónde 'stá la pianola

allí en en rincón oscuro
'stán mis tres camaradas
 el conejo
 el huesudo
 y el fatasma

le 'stán entrando duro
a vironga
y vironga
y más vironga

nomás saludo a los chavos
y me voy de pasada
hoy me siento gacho
y quiero 'star solo
con mi dolor

pongo 3 rolas
 la cama de piedra
 el huérfano
 y 'stoy en el rincón diuna cantina

y me tiro
pa' una mesa
onde no hay ninguna cara
y empiezo
con otra
y otra vironga

3.

poco a poco siento
como el piso sucio
y las sillas y mesas roñosas
comienzan a'garrar un color

muy de aquellas
y pido otra y otra vironga
y el mundo comienza a dar vuelta y vuelta
como una lucecita
en zurco lleno de agua

y entonces me comienza
a salir un chorro de caracajadas
por la boca
orejas
y ojos
y siento que por fin se comienza
a'flojar una espina
muy grande que traigo
en el corazón

4.

es la espina
del gringo dueño de toda esta tierra
del gringo con casa de 2 pisos
del gringo con 3 carros
del gringo que 2 veces por año
va'vacaciones a europa

del gringo que fue jefe de mi abuelo
de apá y que ahora a mi me sigue
pagando con mierda

del gringo que día tras semana tras año
va'cabando con mi vida

del gringo que un día destos
como hay un dios
va'pagar con su vida

Esperando en el hospital

leo los poemas tercermundistas
de reyes cárdenas
my friend from seguín, tejas

& pace up and down
the hospital corridors
& look out
the ventanas chorreadas

there are things
that happen so suddenly

de repente 'stá nublado
luego sale el sol
entonces cai nieve
y vuelve en friega el sol
& melts the snow
todo esto within the hour

there are things
that happen so suddenly

but here we just wait
& wait

the sick kids cry & get sicker
the adults bicker & get impatient

but there are things
that happen so suddenly

los headlines smeared with baby vomit
dicen que there was a riot at the state pen
órale pues
many died
en el desmadre por todos lados

y los pintos took over
& were in command of their lives
& it all happened so suddenly

so suddenly
puro pedo
for generations they've grown tired
of the inhuman conditions that don't change

estoy con ustedes camaradas
porque son gente pobre
y los pobres siempre son aplastados

there are things
that happen so suddenly

pero aquí en el county hospital
está toda mi gente enferma
esperando y esperando
cuz the poor always have to wait

i pace up & down
the corridors
then read reyes cárdenas' poem
about the triumph
of the sandinistas in nicaragua

i glance
at mi compañera
que está toda preocupada
holding our little one
con una temperatura of 104º

y llegan y se van las horas
y entran y salen los doctores
with their cups of coffee
& sarcastic laughs
& hypocritic side-glances

& all of us wait
cuz the poor man always waits
& gets stepped-on
& waits & waits

til he won't take the abuses
no more
y explota en revolución

yes there are things
that seem to happen so suddenly

Frío

cama caliente
de pechos y piernas hirvientes
de la que más quiero
calientes colchas
caliente éxtasis
y despertamos tejidos
y mis manos enloquecidas
recorren tu largo pelo

que caliente está bajo tu piel
y que fría esta mañana nuevo mejicana
y que agüite
tener que surgir de tus labios calientes
de tí
lo que más quiero
y tener que enfrentarme
al conjelado mundo capitalista
pidiendo jale pa' hacerla

doy un brinco de chapulín
y me clavo los tramos fríos
lisa fría
calcetines fríos
y calcos casi conjelados

no hay calentadores en la casa
ni en el carro descompuesto
ni en el barrio
parece que en estos tiempos duros
nomás los ricos mantienen verija caliente
y pienso en tu respiración
y tu estómago caliente
mientras pongo agua conjelada en mi cara
y le rayo la madre
a los dueños del mundo
a quien tengo que pedir jale pa' hacerla

prendo una vela en el cuarto
de los niños
y los persino
con la cruz de quetzalcoatl
y les digo por entre dientes conjelados
que cueste lo que cueste
la vamos a hacer
y los tapo bien
con la pila de colchas conjeladas

abro la puerta de la cocina
y me da una patada
el aire conjelado
y lucho tanto para detener
el pensamiento de tus labios calientes
por toda mi cara
y te quiero más que nunca
al mirar el cielo conjelado

y ahora camino con patas conjeladas
por un camino conjelado
donde me esperan
las frías caras capitalistas
a quien tengo que pedir jale pa hacerla
caras frías gabachas que controlan mi mundo
caras frías ricas
que guardan verijas calientes
todo este invierno conjelado

Pigmemory

you say i'm a pig
a fascist pig of mind & actions
a pig in a world controlled by pigs
& that my kind of pig
was meant to be roasted

and your words as knife plunge
into my gut
then rip to spill my insides

órale pues
i see your need to go all the way
aunque tu coraje
ha enchuecado tu perspectiva

and i ask you to spare the head
as you start skinning me
your knifing words getting sharper
with the momentum of the blood flow

órale pues
aviéntate
porque era inevitable
pero no cortes la cabeza
porque ahí cargo la memoria
de todo lo que he visto

y te encabronas más
y me odias más
and you say that when you kill a pig
you kill him all over
and with one blow
of your arthritic arm
you cut it all

perhaps you're right
maybe all pigs should be butchered
pero debes saber
que yo nunca quise ser marrano
así nací
y así me crió la sociedad

en realidad
yo siempre quise ser un caballo
a powerful horse with wide nostrils
that can take in lots of air
with powerful hind legs
that can break the pull of gravity
and jump into space
pa' respirar el aire puro
y ver todo desde allá
and gallop so fast without impediments
that i would gradually dissolve

me entiendes compañera
to be pure animal energy
por un instante
pa' luego regresar a los barrios del mundo
y galopear por la vida sufrida
más fuerte que nunca

pero dices que soy marrano
and pigs are born to be fattened in pigpens
and then butchered
y ahora has cortado
la memoria de mi vida
& piglife though it was
still it was the only thing i knew

y ahora qué
me comerás con tu coraje
or will you feed me to the dogs
will you hang my choice parts to dry out

or will you turn me into chicharrones y tamales
i guess not
cuz that ain't your style
or is it

sabes que lo cierto es que
i just don't know who the hell you are
this thing happened too soon for me
no hubo tiempo pa' resolver las cosas

you tabulated todos los choques
too accurately and with a twist
to justify the kill
and yeah all pigs
have to be butchered

the only pig one can get close to
is the dead pig

órale pues
y ahora supongo que estás contenta

don't forget to mop-up the blood
porque si no se va a llenar tu vida de moscas

the only thing that worries me
about all this
is what your knifing words
will do to my memory

that's what you're going to keep with you
for last
yes
what you hated the most
verdad
my pigmemory
as you always used to say

Space

i feel the gabacho eyes
like blue pus
on my body

the leader
opens his mouth
& the forked-tongue
darts through the fangs
as he whips at me
a cynical laugh

breathing deep
i hold my space
against the invasion

they are trying to make me feel
as small as a pile of shit
they butcher me with laser words
then spit at my soul

but i hold my space
breathing evenly
against the centuries of oppression

y les digo otra vez
in my broken chicano english

que aquí es aztlán
que aquí nacimos
que aquí es nuestra casa
que todavía estamos resistiendo
la conquista europea

they are hating me
with their abusive fears

as i breathe into my space
& hold my space

against the racism
& ignorance
of these brothers

portrait for mamá

mamá's sculptured hands
grind deer meat

in a while the old ladies will be here
to make tamales for tomorrow's celebration

she's been at it for hours
singing the old folk songs
that give her the strength
papá took when he abandoned us

i never tire of looking at her
and right now it's the power
of her workingclass pianist hands
that's helping me draw into these eyes
the compassion to see the very soul of humanity

the saturday sun suddenly overwhelms with light
our rundown kitchen

mamá bellylaughs and sings louder her song
about picking cotton all day

she dances to my desk and eating table
and caresses my face
with her translucent hands

and now i'm going to sing for our neighbors
she says and laughs her whole body out the door

it's being close to her presence
her waves of voluptuous black hair
that always helps to make things happen

and now i've finished and i call it
count leo tolstoi my father
looking into the depths of katerina maslova

it's for your tiny room mamá
just as the song you're singing on the porch
is your gift of hope and joy
to our poor neighborhood

3/10/1983

gris

'stá tan empapado de gris el día
que no se watcha la montaña
ni los barrioboys que duermen
en el montecito al otro la'o del chante
despúes de las pedas locas

grises las caras de la gente
que va avocanada pa' los jales

gris mi cuerpo feo
y la ropa que lo cubre

and the clinging chafo thoughts
grises también
tan grises que'l camino
que me lleva a las caras grises
de las abogadas pa' quien trabajo

grises las traiciones de rucas chisquiadas
que se juntan like gris cancer of the gut

grises las mentes de los niños
with alcoholic fathers

gris es la pobreza
of the freezing street people
who drag about in this godless
gris cycle of desmadre

gris tu recuerdo
gris mi ansiedad

gris the heart
pumping sangre gris
en esta mañana nuevomexicana

respiro hondamente con mis pulmones entristecidos
then exhale un gris histórico con mal olor

y mi gris y el gris del mundo
se mezclan en un grito sufrido y frío
que retumba por la jaula gris en que vivimos

eight o'clock downtown gris
and the grey tension
of making it on time traps us

parecemos psychotic ratas grises
gris entre lo más gris
like the gris smile
i feel creeping around my face

1/30/1986

from Talking to the Rio Grande

SIEMPRE REGRESO A TI, my source, you gnarled piece of liquid leather. When I feel good or reventado you're always there for me. Solamente your indifference tiene la capacidad de entender the outpourings of my soul. As a child in Laredo I knew you as the powerful divider of a people who were once one and the same, y ahora de aquel lado están los mexicanos, y acá, nosotros, los tejanos. You flowed on doing your thing, not caring about the weird games men play. I swam in you and your dark waters mixed with my blood. Toda mi vida he permanecido cerca de ti 'cause I have the need to reveal myself to you so that I can cope con todas las chingaderas de la vida. Listen to me old one, and help me make her love me once again . . .

¿Pero cómo jodidos le hago para resolver la situación? Old river, how can I reject with my body la maña of wanting to own her? ¿Cómo puedo dejar de ser lo que soy? How? I'd have to die and be reborn. If I were a rattlesnake and could change skins I'd be renewed. I'd be young with a glistening new skin. I'd drink your waters with a new soul. Maybe then I wouldn't have the need of wanting her by my side. I'd even be able to forgive my father. To be renewed, but first I'd have to die.

I almost died once, remember? Yes, I was in junior high, and my friends from school and I played hookey, and I took them in my old car to the family ranch. Man, aquellos sí eran tiempos locotes. And then I showed them something special, la noria, so deep and mysterious. I remember my cousins Kiko and Pepé digging it years before, and I was always afraid to get close to it. But now my friends were right up to the rim of the well, and they saw some snakes at the bottom. They got all excited and started shooting at them with two .22-caliber rifles. I yelled no, son víboras negras, they're harmless. Están allá abajo porque hay ratas y se las van a comer. But they just kept shooting like maniacs. Then they argued about who was going to go down the ladder to get the snakes so we could take them back to Laredo and scare the shit out of people, but nobody had the guts to volunteer. Then someone said I should go down 'cause after all it was my ranch and I was used to those kinds of things, and they circled me and called me joto, miedoso, chicken shit and pussy. My heart started jumping all over the place, but I decided to go down anyway. I'd show them que mi verga estaba más gruesa than all of theirs put together. I started going down and it felt warm, with a tightness then a release, as if the dark and damp well were pulsating. There was a thick old smell all around. I could barely see the bottom, but I knew the snakes were dead, probably killed twenty times over. I went lower, trying to focus on the snakes. The well now felt cool and exhilarating. Suddenly I saw a movement all around me. I couldn't believe that the dark walls were moving all around me. Then I realized there were thousands of crickets living there and the shooting had agitated them. I stood still and looked at them for a moment. They were like a black blanket moving in waves. Then my friends again me rayaron la madre and even threw stones, and I felt so alone and scared. The crickets got more excited when my foot slipped and I almost fell. With one hand I braced myself against the wall of the well, but when I did that the crickets began jumping. I felt their cool and spiny legs all over my body, and then they started chirping, first a few chirping softly, then more. I had my balance now, then by the thousands the crickets were chirping louder and louder all around me. Their song relaxed me, and I did not feel scared of them any more. It seemed as if they were playing their cricket song so that I wouldn't hear my drunk father or my friends yelling obscenities. I didn't care about falling off the ladder or about the snakes. The rhythm of the crickets' song kept coming into me, filling up my mind and every part of my body like a soothing dream. I knew my face was smiling, yes, I was at peace with myself for the first time in my life, and at that moment that's all that mattered in the world. The song of the crickets and I became one.

foto 1

un filtro pretende obfuscar
las emociones del mundo

mientras tú repites en tonos grises
el juego con las muñecas en la cama

claude monet's waterlilies
are splattered about in books
but the erotic colors can't touch you

tan cerca de ti
que pudiera acariciar tus pechos

sigo tratando de entender la técnica
the particular exposure
of you're shattered past
y la manera obsesiva
con que manipulas las muñecas

that's always been your problem
dices enfadada
you can't feel things
cause you're too busy
trying to understand them

you used to like that about me

pues ya no

i'm trying to understand your addiction
at least give me credit for that

there you go again
chinga'o cómo jodes
just get the hell out

it's too hot and humid out there

well the fucking humidity
is sticking to your brains
and you're driving me crazy

you're not crazy
you just need more crack
admit it

fuck you

is that all you can say

fuck you

ok i'm off into the humidity
see you later

i drink some more beer
and focus on the floating mirror

i have you against the wall
with a knife at your throat
y te grito pinche vieja traicionera

you don't have the guts to do it
ya te lo dije
i am what i am
acéptame or get the hell out

it's getting late
i need to go out for a walk
maybe get some more beer
get a glimpse
of the snow-covered mountain
to help me sort out old angers
to tell myself i'm still ready

for the moment of understanding
that can shed a little light
on the damn bits of memory
that like chains
keep tossing around the head

hot humid days have a tendency
to distort our frenzied thoughts
de todo lo que pudo ser

lo dijo ella esa tarde
del desmadre final
o lo acabo de pensar yo

que importa
it's a good line

2 enero 1991

foto 10

the trail winds
through dry sunflowers
and suddenly unfolds
the skeletal forest of cottonwoods
with its undulating sea of shadows

i must go on
in spite of accumulated fears

at a given moment
can the one who threatens
be more scared than the threatened

can writing poetry
ever be as easy as breathing

does my relationship with her
keep me from understanding myself

an erratic reflection
pursues my steps
and i understand it's coming from a gun
demanding my attention

it's either the philosopher
of the pervert
who wants to shoot me

if it's the pervert i'll die
because i'm witness
to his abuse of the family name

if it's the philosopher
i'll know at the last moment
of the eternal deception of words

pero puede ser ella
with her short masculine hair
wide hips
seductive mouth
and tattooed arms

you can't leave me
if you do i'll kill you

but can't you understand
you're killing both of us

i'll change

you can't

fuck you

that won't solve the problem

but i love you

you love the drugs more

but i need you

no you need my salary

give me another chance

i've given you a thousand

what will i do

seguirás destruyéndote

where will i go

the choice is yours
i say extending my arm
to the four directions of the world

you sonofabitch

te seguiré amando

i'll kill you

nunca te olvidaré

in a moment
the quivering blackness of the shadows
will swallow the winter sun

two fat shreds of clouds roll around
in the monstrous blue silence

the insistent reflection
dances off the gun

and as i walk on
accepting the inevitability of fear
three blue jays swoop
in front of me
and take my breath away

i could photograph them forever
gliding around a glistening gun barrel
around dancing shadows
around a selfdoubting philosopher
an insecure pervert
and my demon-infested amada

yes the one who betrays me
la que maldice mi ser
la que me inspira eternamente

28 october 1991

dream 4

i'm about 30
as i stand by my father's deathbed

he's got all kinds of tubes
coming out of his wasted body

gasping for breath
he says he wants to have a final talk
pero le contesto que no podemos
porque no sabemos conversar

i walk away quickly
porque ahora sospecho
que quiere cobrar venganza
because he thinks i'm not his son

when i'm about 19
mamá dances in the livingroom

le explico que su devotion
to an alcoholic is irrational

for the last time
i'm asking you to leave him

how can i
in spite of everything i love him
please accept my decision

but the suffering
of this situation is too much

then accept my suffering
and i'll accept yours

but can't you see
he's killing all of us

again do you really want to go
through all this again
i told you i've made my decision
she says and continues dancing

pero mamá

can't you see i'm dancing
please leave me alone

i'm about 10
and papá is getting ready
to gamble in hell

from behind the curtain
i can tell he's sober
and in a good mood

when mamá brings him a beer
he squeezes her butt
and grunts like a chivo

then his friends come in
and they drink and gamble
for hours

everyone gets drunk
and they cheat
argue
vomit
and finally leave screaming babosadas

papá then cusses mamá
because he lost money

you're bad luck
all my fucking life
you've been nothing
but bad luck

it's not true
why do you say that

cause it's fucking true
you cling to me
like a fucking bug

you're drunk
and tired
please go to bed

bed my ass pendeja
you're the reason
i can't get ahead in life

mide tu lengua

you and the fucking kids
tie me down
i hate you
and the one
that's not mine

y si no es tuyo
de quién es
a ver dime

how the fuck
should i know
i was in the war

y yo estaba aquí
esperándote con tu hijo

que pinche suerte
i could've gone to college
with the g i bill

no quisiste
i wanted you to
pero no quisiste

and who was gonna feed
you and all your fucking kids

son nuestros hijos
los dos los hicimos

you can't do shit
you're a dumb bitch
that just knows
how to get pregnant
that's all the shit you know

mentiroso andas borracho
y no sabes lo que dices

when mamá calls him
a drunken liar he hits her in the face
y cuando cae al piso
le da una patada

mamá bleeds profusely
and the boy walks away

he wishes the moon
was not fat and shiny
so he could cry harder

it's always easier
to cry the heart out
in total darkness

11/5/1987

dream 6

the house turns into
a disfigured ball of fire

the wild horses mamá bought
with papá's war salary
gallop around the fire
and lick the flames

i sit a few yards away
writing my last letter

to the one and only woman
i truly loved

no
that never really happened
scratch it out

to the one and only teacher
i ever respected

no
he was really a scumbag
who read poetry
scratch it out

to my one and only father
yes that's it

dear papá
we should've tried
to have a relationship

it's hard not knowing
who you were

the horses are now on fire
they spin around
and laugh hysterically

one of them snorts a flame
que galopea por la mesa
y se me sube por un brazo
y baja por el otro

i put it out
and continue writing

what can i do
with the pain papá
do you have any suggestions

the house and the horses
burn furiously

i know i won't finish the letter
before everything turns into ashes

and i try to understand
why the bedroom window
por donde entra
y sale mi mundo
hasn't burned

it hangs there
surrounded by fire

i wonder what kept me
from seeing it before

7/31/1989

dream 8

the roof of the old morada
has rotted away

the once plastered walls
now reveal countless piled stones
charged with the accumulated power
of the songs

through a frameless window
i sense the lacerated souls
of the brotherhood

i hear the soft whispering
of a million birds

a blue pickup arrives
with the first ray of the sun

a woman quickly gets out
and props a tripod
by the front door of the morada

she returns to the truck
and emerges as a tiny girl
with a guitar

who walks into the morada
and sits in front
of the decaying altar
and plays the old songs

the music circles
around the morada
around the old cemetery
around the silent birds
and around my heart

where it finally settles
as a small pile
of effervescent dust

the little girl
returns to the pickup
and walks out
again in her early 30s

she carries a large camera
which she places on the tripod

and then photographs
each and every part of the morada

when she finishes
she lights up a red candle
and places it on a broken crate
in front of the altar

the birds pray in unison
until the candle burns out

at home in the city
her legs are wide apart
and a man moves inside her

she returns the intensity
of his thrusts
by biting his neck

and letting the wings
of her frenzy
fly her to a turbulent climax

dust to dust
and passion in-between

i'm not a separate person
at this moment
she whispers in his ear

but a thousand birds
singing the mystery
of the soul

then she glances
at the eternal window
that frames
the black and white photograph
of the ancient morada
that is still turning
to sacred dust

9/5/1989

dream 9

i notice the tracks
of the herd of cows
all over my body

as i run under the mid-day sun
sweating profusely
to disguise my agenda

running along the river
i am a giant
crushing houses with every step

the screams
of people and animals
fuel my insatiable quest for power

i step into a barn
tucked away in a damp cave
and wave to the multitude of cows

they continue chewing
as i address them

ladies and gentlemen
i've done a lot of running
to come here and tell you
why i want to be
your next governor

mooooo

i'll come straight
to the point of my platform

mooooo

power dear folks

mooooo

yes
i want the power
i need to crush the disgusting dark side
of my memory

mooooo

certainly all of you
can understand that

mooooo

can i count on your vote then
will you vote for me

mooooo

9/14/1989

dream 11

a giant golden snake
coils under the noon shade
of the cottonwood

opens wide his jaws
and regurgitates a massive warm egg

on a large bed
with the whitest sheets

a speckled egg
which vibrates
then cracks

a baby's arm thrusts out
then the tiny feathered head
with a current of nurturing sounds

running
breathing deeply up the snake
that is the mountain path

i hear its cold
and scaly breathing

and feel my shoulder blades
sprout wings
damp wings
that expand powerfully

from the top of the mountain
the snake drum calls
like a heartbeat
and i continue chanting

ho ay va mos ya ya va mos ho
ho ay va mos ya ya va mos ho

10/15/1989

dream 12

someone stole my photograph
between 1:30 and 3:00 pm

it was either mamá
or my exwife

i've got to find them
and get my photo

i go out the back door
and into a long semidark corridor

i finally find a door
which opens
and there's another corridor
another door
another corridor

this is sickening i think
as i see a window
with flickering lights

i peek at a tiny baby
who's asleep
and surrounded by candles

i try to open the window
to pick up the baby
when i see a cop
who shouts at me
hold it right there
don't move motherfucker

i move towards the nearest door
and run out

to cross
a busy street

but a pickup hits me
drags me on my face
then speeds off

most of my face
is dangling
like a rag

one of my eyeballs
has popped out

with my good eye
i barely make out a woman
who looks at me
and screams

she clutches my photo
but i black out
and can't figure out
if it's mamá or my ex

i wake up in the hospital
with broken legs and arms

they've sewed up the eye
with the missing eyeball
and straightened up my face
so it looks human

but since most of the facial bone
was pulverized
there's a hole
from my mouth
to the forehead

my mouth
there's a big gadget in it
to help me with the breathing

thank god i at least have
an eye that works

let's see
according to the medical chart
my lungs are swollen
and accumulating fluid

if this continues
i'll drown

fuck
why the fuck
don't they put in a big needle
with a hose
and drain out my lungs

i've got to relax
otherwise my eye
gets blurry

i can hardly see
but now someone places
the photograph
on the food tray

let's see
she has a ring
with coral and turquoise stones

damn it
i gave both mamá
and my ex identical rings

she's leaving

i wish she'd wait

she hesitates
then grabs the photo
and runs out

i'm about to scream
when i remember the gadget
in my mouth
and for all i know
i might have lost my tongue

i'll never see the photo again
qué pinche suerte

the nurse just came in
so i've closed
my blurry good eye

that's the best plan
i can think of

10/24/1989

dream 14

the body wrapped in plastic
is in back of the van
and now i'm heading south

it's badly decomposed
and i wonder if the border guards
will be able to smell it

i stop by the side of the road
to piss

but when i open the door
a herd of goats jumps in

they are voraciously hungry
and quickly eat the seatcovers

the rearview mirror tells me
they're also eating the plastic bag
and decomposed body

they tear at my clothing
and now they're going to eat me
and i can't make a run for it

i look at my watch
to see what time i'm going to die
but instead of numbers
i see i'm by the river
under my favorite cottonwood

she teases me by lifting her dress

aha no panties

i kneel in front of her
and kiss her vagina

she groans with pleasure
then pushes me away

a man in black suit
and black hat approaches us

he waves a knife at me
then ties me against the tree

he's drunk out of his mind
and grunts like an animal

he then fucks her savagely
right on the sand
all the time waving the knife
in her face

she cries harder
throughout his orgasm
bleeding from both cheeks

then he stands and orders her
to shut up
but she can't

fucking bitch
he grunts
and grabs a huge rock
and smashes her face

i go into convulsions
and cuss him out

then for the first time
notice his big black moustache

he laughs
then sticks the knife in my mouth

tears and blood from the palate
stain my t-shirt
with the huelga eagle

i'm not gonna kill you faggot
a little suffering is good for you
he says then walks away

i manage to untie myself
take a last look
at what's left of her face
then wrap her in plastic
and put her over my shoulder

i better go south
just keep going south
following the river

i wonder if the border guards
will take her away from me

i look around the big blue sky
and can't locate the sun
but it sure is as hot as hell

i'm sure she'll decompose
by the time i get there

i wonder if i'll be able to stand the smell

11/12/1989

3824

98